Praise for
A New Buddhist Path

"In this new book, Zen teacher, sage, and activist David Loy offers a fresh Buddhist perspective for a post-Axial age that addresses and challenges adherents of any religion or no religion, as we together face the gravest crises of our history. *A New Buddhist Path* lays out the contours of a liberating spiritual practice, a new story, and an integral vision that links personal transformation with wholehearted engagement toward healing our deeply wounded and fragmented Earth community."

—Ruben L. F. Habito, author of *Living Zen, Loving God*

"This gripping, important, and ultimately heartening book by David Loy is a wake-up call for Buddhists and everyone else on how to respond to current crises."

—Lila Kate Wheeler, author of *When Mountains Walked*

"Any book by David Loy makes me sit up and take notice. A favorite Buddhist voice, he reliably brightens my day by giving me confidence in our capacity to preserve the precious gift of life.

"This breathtakingly insightful book captures what the Buddha-dharma most distinctively brings to this apocalyptic moment in our crisis-ridden world. For one like me, who loves the Buddha's teachings with the same heart that grew up loving Hebrew prophets and Jesus, and the same mind that peered at his Dharma through the lens of systems science, David Loy's presentation of 'A New Path' is both trustworthy and thrilling. I have always counted on David Loy for his explication of the systemic, institutionalized forms of greed, hatred, and delusion, the 'three poisons' now threatening all life on Earth. With this treasure of a book I equally prize his wide-angle reflections on collective awakening and his good, grounding presentation of the bodhisattva archetype, so meaningful to so many today, Buddhists and non-Buddhists alike."

—Joanna Macy, author of *Coming Back to Life*

A New Buddhist Path

A New Buddhist Path

Path

enlightenment

evolution

and ethics

in the

modern world

David R. Loy

Wisdom Publications • Boston

Wisdom Publications
199 Elm Street
Somerville, MA 02144 USA
www.wisdompubs.org

Library of Congress Cataloging-in-Publication Data
Loy, David, 1947– author.
  A new Buddhist path : enlightenment, evolution, and ethics in the modern world / David R. Loy.
    pages cm
  Includes bibliographical references and index.
  ISBN 1-61429-002-4 (pbk. : alk. paper) — ISBN 978-1-61429-003-2 (Ebook)
  1. Buddhism—Social aspects. 2. Buddhist philosophy. I. Title.
  BQ4570.S6L72 2015
  294.3'42--dc23

                    2014020917

ISBN 978-1-61429-002-5   ebook ISBN 978-1-61429-003-2

19 18 17 16 15
5 4 3 2 1

Cover design by Philip Pascuzzo. Interior design by Gopa&Ted2, Inc. Set in Whitman 11.2/15.25.

Wisdom Publications' books are printed on acid-free paper and meet the guidelines for permanence and durability of the Production Guidelines for Book Longevity of the Council on Library Resources.

This book was produced with environmental mindfulness. We have elected to print this title on 30% PCW recycled paper. As a result, we have saved the following resources: 11 trees, 5 million BTUs of energy, 988 lbs. of greenhouse gases, 5,358 gallons of water, and 356 lbs. of solid waste. For more information, please visit our website, www.wisdompubs.org.

Printed in the United States of America.

Please visit www.fscus.org.

To the new bodhisattvas

TABLE OF CONTENTS

Introduction:
In Quest of a Modern Buddhism   1

Path   9

Transcendence?   10

The Problem with Transcendence   19

The Problem with Immanence   26

Mindfulness   33

Beyond Transcendence and Immanence   39

Constructing the Self and Its World   41

Nonattachment   47

Letting Go   51

Something Infinite Behind Everything   54

Implications   62

Story   65

A Devalued World   67

Social Darwinism   68

Creation Stories 73

A New Evolutionary Myth 76

A New Buddhist Story 86

Progress 90

Creatures that Create 94

The Meaning of It All 97

A Pivotal Stage 100

Challenge 105

Good vs. Evil 107

Ignorance vs. Awakening 113

The Economic Challenge 118

The Ecological Challenge 123

The New Bodhisattva 126

Conclusion:
Reflections on Karma and Rebirth 135

Acknowledgments 145

Recommended Books 147

Index 151

About the Author 165

INTRODUCTION:

In Quest of a Modern Buddhism

"MAY YOU LIVE in interesting times," says the apocryphal Chinese curse, and for those on a Buddhist path these times are doubly interesting. As Buddhism spreads to the West (or to the modern world, since "the West" is globalizing), Buddhism is encountering its greatest challenge ever: the most successful civilization in human history, whose powerful technologies and formidable institutions offer apparently limitless possibilities along with unprecedented perils.

The naturalistic worldview and materialistic values of the modern world are quite different from what Buddhism traditionally has to offer—and they also appear increasingly problematic and vulnerable, due to deeply rooted ecological, economic, and social crises that modernity has created but seems unable to resolve. Our predicament calls for new perspectives that question many of its priorities and presuppositions.

In a conversation not long before his death, the British historian Arnold Toynbee reflected that "The present threat to mankind's survival can be removed only by a revolutionary change of heart in individual human beings. This change of heart must be inspired by religion in order to generate the willpower needed for putting arduous new ideals into practice." Does this help us to understand his reputed prediction that the introduction of Buddhism to the West "may well prove to be the most important event of the twentieth century"?

that the introduction of Buddhism to the West "may well prove to be the most important event of the twentieth century"?

Whenever Buddhism has spread to a new culture, it has interacted with the indigenous traditions of that society, and the result of their encounter has been something better suited to that culture. Each is changed by the other—and there is no reason to suspect that anything different is happening today: it is a safe bet that the contemporary conversation between Buddhism and the modern world will lead to the development of new forms of Buddhism particularly adapted for the members of an emerging global civilization.

Yet that predictable result does not in itself clarify the role that Buddhism will play within this civilization. Will Buddhist temples and Dharma centers adapt to modern life by helping us cope with the stress of surviving in a deteriorating ecological and economic climate? Or will we appreciate Buddhist teachings and practices because they offer a radically different worldview, with an alternative perspective on what's happening now and what needs to be done? Or do we need both?

As these reflections suggest, the issue is not only what Buddhism can offer to modernity, but just as much what modernity offers to Buddhism. Before Buddhism came to the West, the West came to Buddhism, thanks to European imperialism and missionary proselytizing. It turned out to be a salutary wake-up call. The Mahayana scholar Edward Conze said that Buddhism hasn't had an original idea in a thousand years. Although I'm dubious about his dates—in the thirteenth century Zen master Dogen revolutionized traditional ways of conceptualizing the Dharma—Conze's basic point remains a challenge to Buddhism even if it applies only to the last seven hundred years. Is the encounter with modernity the best thing that has happened to Buddhism in a very long time?

THIS BOOK OUTLINES the basic features of a contemporary Buddhism that tries to be both faithful to its most important traditional teachings and also compatible with modernity, or at least with many of the most characteristic elements of the modern worldview. Despite the ambitious title, the pages that follow inevitably offer a personal perspective on some aspects of the dialogue so far. They do not address the implications of recent discoveries in neuroscience, nor academic work in the field of cognitive science. And of course the interactions that I do address are, if not quite beginning, still in their early days. There is no question of providing a new version of Buddhism that will stand the test of time. Instead, the best that any of us can hope for is to contribute to the ongoing conversation, in the belief that a collective wisdom is beginning to emerge, which will be something more than the sum of separate voices.

THE MAIN CHALLENGE to developing a modern Buddhism is the difficulty of achieving a genuine dialogue that is not predisposed to evaluate one side in terms of the other.

On the traditional side, for the last few generations the main concern has naturally been to import particular schools of Asian Buddhism and foster support for them. Such a conventional approach might be summarized as follows: "Some adjustments need to be made, of course, but without conceding any significant alteration in the basic teachings and ways of practicing. That such traditions are premodern is not a weakness but their strength, given what the modern world has become and where it seems to be going. The prevalent Western worldview promotes individualism and narcissism, its economic system encourages greed, and society as a whole seems to be entranced in consumerist addictions and fantasies. We need to revitalize this ancient wisdom that can point us back in the right direction."

On the other side, however, the main concern is to make Buddhism more relevant to contemporary society by secularizing it, replacing its Iron Age mythological roots with a worldview more compatible with science and other modern ways of knowing. "Sure, modernity has its problems, but we must build on the best of what it has discovered. This includes not only hard sciences such as physics and biology but also social sciences such as psychology and sociology. Instead of accepting premodern beliefs that are no longer plausible today, we can also benefit from what anthropology and archaeology, for example, have learned about ancient ways of thinking. Only that approach can develop a Buddhism that speaks directly to our situation today—the dis-ease of modern people living in a globalizing world."

Sympathizing with both perspectives is easy; walking the knife-edge between them is more difficult. Can we employ each viewpoint to interrogate the other, without accepting either perspective as absolute? Such an approach can be discomforting because it is so destabilizing: what remains of one's own standpoint? This process invokes the understanding of Buddhist practice discussed in part I, which emphasizes the realization of "nondwelling mind": a mind that does not identify with any particular forms, including thought-forms such as ideologies, whether religious or secular.

Although the Asian Buddhist traditions continue to fascinate many of us, clearly we need to distinguish the essentials of the Dharma from cultural trappings that don't fit as well into the modern world—do those include karma and rebirth? Yet a secularized Buddhism may assume some of the very things that a Buddhist perspective might critique as problematic. Does the prevalent materialist worldview of modern science express the truth of the world we live in, or has it become questionable—as some distinguished scientists, including Nobel laureate physicists and biologists, now believe? Differentiating science as a methodology from the dominant naturalistic paradigm opens the door to new conceptions of what this world is and to a fresh understanding of our place and role within it, which are discussed in part II.

ONE OF THE CRUCIAL ISSUES for contemporary Buddhism is enlightenment: *nibbana* in Pali, *nirvana* in Sanskrit, awakening, liberation, realization, etc. Although it's difficult to imagine a Buddhism (literally, "Awake-ism") without it, there is an ambiguity about the nature of enlightenment that is becoming increasingly problematic as Buddhism globalizes and modernizes.

According to some early versions of Buddhism, this world of *samsara* is inherently infested with craving, delusion, and the discontent they cause. The only really satisfactory solution is to escape it by attaining nirvana, which ends rebirth into samsara. This approach is consistent with other Axial Age religions (including Abrahamic ones such as Judaism, Christianity, and Islam) that also emphasize *transcending* (from the Latin *trans* + *scandere*, "to climb over or surmount") this world.

In contrast, some contemporary versions of Buddhism understand the Buddhist path as a program of psychological development that helps us cope with personal problems, especially the "monkey mind" and its afflictive emotions. The influence of psychotherapy has led to a greater appreciation of entrenched mental problems and relationship difficulties, which traditional Buddhist practices do not always address well. The mindfulness movement is another promising development, but, like psychotherapy, such perspectives on Buddhism tend to emphasize accepting and adapting to this world. Throughout this book I will refer to this approach as *immanent* (from Latin *in* + *manere*, "to dwell in, remain in"). Although such therapeutic and mindfulness practices have much to offer, do they nevertheless overlook other important dimensions of the Dharma?

Part I argues that neither a transcendent nor an immanent understanding of Buddhism is satisfactory, given what we know today and what we need today. This section offers an alternative version of the path and its goal: the sense of self is a psychological and social construct that can be deconstructed and reconstructed, and that *needs* to be deconstructed and reconstructed, because the delusion of a separate self is the source of our most problematic *dukkha*, or "suffering." We don't need to attain anything or anywhere else, just to realize the true nature of this world (including ourselves) here and now—which involves a more nondual way of experiencing that is quite different from merely accepting this world as it is, or as it seems to be.

That the self is a construct accords with what developmental psychology has discovered, but a Buddhist constructivism opens the door to possibilities that modernity has not considered seriously, because those potentials are incompatible with its naturalistic perspective. In that sense, an *awakened* way of experiencing and living in this world can also be described as transcending it, because the alternative that Buddhism offers does indeed transcend our usual dualistic understanding of the world and ourselves within it.

THIS WAY OF describing the Buddhist path and its fruit raises some other important issues. Is the nondualist perspective developed in part I compatible with what modern science has discovered? Or with what contemporary science is discovering now? It seems difficult to reconcile a spiritual path with the materialist and reductionist paradigm that has been so successful in bending the world to our will—a worldview, to say it again, that many scientists themselves now find problematical.

Another issue raised by this way of understanding the Buddhist path is its social and ecological implications. "History is a race between education and catastrophe," according to H. G. Wells, and the race is speeding up, on both sides. Catastrophe may not be too strong a term for the future that has begun to unfold. While global warming (a cozy euphemism for climate breakdown) is happening more quickly than most climate scientists anticipated, our collective efforts to address it remain wholly inadequate. Unless you are a banker or investor, there has been little if any recovery from the Great Recession that began in 2008, and the economic future for recent college graduates looks grim. (Bumper sticker on my car: "If the environment were a bank, we would have saved it by now.") And the political paralysis in Washington looks unlikely to end soon, because it reflects a fragmentation in our national consciousness.

At the same time, something else is struggling to be born. Paul Hawken's book *Blessed Unrest: How the Largest Social Movement in History Is Restoring Grace, Justice, and Beauty to the World* was inspired by his realization that something historically unprecedented is happening today: an extraordinary number of organizations, large and small, have sprung up to work for peace, social justice, and sustainability. His original estimate was between one million and one and a half million, but since then he has determined that the true number must be well over two million. "Sprung up" is the appropriate verb, because this movement is not organized top-down: groups are mostly independent, with their own leaders and without any unifying ideology. It reflects a transformation in our collective consciousness that may be just beginning, a change that globalizing Buddhism is part of—and might perhaps even become an important part of.

If awakening involves transcending this suffering world, we can ignore its problems because we are destined for a better place. If the Buddhist path is psychological therapy, we can continue to focus on our own individual neuroses. Yet both of those approaches assume and reinforce the illusion—the basic problem, at the root of our dissatisfaction—that each of us is essentially separate from others, and therefore can be indifferent to what is happening to others and to the world generally.

The challenges that confront us today call upon us to do more than help other individuals deconstruct their own sense of separation (the traditional bodhisattva role). The highest ideal of the modern Western tradition has been to restructure our societies so they become more socially just. The most important Buddhist goal is to awaken and (to use the Zen phrase) realize one's true nature. Today it has become more obvious that we need both: not just because these ideals complement each other, but because those two types of liberation need each other. That relationship between personal transformation and social transformation is explored in part III.

PATH

We are here to awaken
from the illusion of our separateness.

—Thich Nhat Hanh

At the heart of Buddhist teachings there is a crucial ambiguity. It is not a new problem: an ambivalence is apparent even in some of the earliest Buddhist texts, as preserved in the Pali Canon. As Buddhism globalizes and becomes part of the modern world, however, this ambiguity is becoming increasingly awkward. It needs to be resolved for the Buddhist tradition to fulfill its liberative potential—not only to promote individual awakening more successfully, but also to help us address ecological and social challenges that cannot be evaded.

Gautama Buddha said that he simply taught dukkha and how to end it; the four noble (or "ennobling") truths are all about dukkha, what causes it, its cessation, and how to end it. *Dukkha* is usually translated as "suffering," yet that works only if we understand suffering in the broadest sense, to include anxiety and dissatisfaction generally. Why are we haunted by a gnawing dis-ease that keeps us from enjoying our lives? The ambiguity at stake in Buddhism is directly connected with how we understand the source of our dukkha: is the basic problem the nature of this world itself, or our inability to accept it as it is? Or something else?

In early Buddhism, the "end of suffering" is nirvana, which literally means something like "blown out" or "cooled off." But it's not completely clear what those metaphors actually refer to, because the Buddha described the nature of nirvana mostly with negatives (the end of craving, ignorance, etc.) and other metaphors (the shelter, harbor, refuge, etc.—which still leave us with the question "what sort of refuge?").

His apparent reticence leaves us with the important issue of whether nirvana involves attaining some other dimension of reality that *transcends* this world, or whether it describes an experience that is *immanent* in this world—a state of being that might be understood more psychologically, as (for example) the end of greed, ill will, and delusion in our lives right now. Surely nirvana must be one or the other?

Today that basic ambivalence appears most clearly in the contrast between a reading of the Pali Canon that understands nirvana as an unconditioned (*asamskrta*) realm or dimension, and the recent "psychologization" of American Buddhism, especially in the current popularity of the mindfulness movement. Understanding the difference between these two will help us to see a third possibility, which emphasizes neither transcending this world nor accepting it as it is (or seems to be). Rather, the world as normally experienced—including the way we normally experience ourselves—is a psychological and social construction that can be deconstructed and reconstructed. We don't need to attain anything or anywhere else, or to accept the conventional possibilities that modernity assumes. What we need to do is realize that this world is quite different from our usual assumptions about it and about ourselves.

Transcendence?

The earliest Buddhist teachings were collected into what became the Pali Canon, which is approximately eleven times the length of the Bible. The material presented is so extensive and varied that most generalizations become risky, and this is especially true regarding the nature of nirvana. This book is not the place for a comprehensive analysis of the canon, yet it's important to appreciate some of the inconsistencies in the way that nirvana is described—or what at least appear to be inconsistencies. There are plenty of passages in the Nikayas that seem to support transcendence and perhaps as many that seem to imply immanence. Before getting into that, however, we need to know what we are getting into.

According to tradition, the texts of the Pali Canon were memorized and passed down by word of mouth for at least three hundred years before they were written down. How well they preserve the original words of the historical Buddha, and how much those words have been edited and modified in the process, is a controversy that may be never settled. We like to think that its suttas offer us a direct conduit to what the Buddha actually said, but it's not so simple. Religious doctrines can evolve very quickly, especially in the earliest days, when the institutions devoted to preserving the legacy of the founder are still taking shape. Within a single generation the parables of Jesus, an apocalyptic Jewish prophet, became overshadowed by his new role as resurrected god who can save us—thanks to the extraordinarily successful missionary efforts of Paul, who never met the living Jesus but apparently knew better than anyone else what Jesus really meant. How certain can we be that the compilers of the Pali Canon knew what the Buddha meant and accurately preserved what he taught?

Some of its mythological elements reflect ways of thinking that were generally accepted in the Buddha's time and place (Iron Age India) but are more difficult to credit today. It presents the world as an enchanted place full of supernormal powers and disincarnate spirits. There are stories about the Buddha's conversations with gods and the complaint of a tree spirit whose home had been cut down. We read that the Buddha flew through the air and hovered cross-legged above a river to stop a battle between two armies. In another incident, after a debate the Buddha suddenly rose up into the air and flew away. He also ascended to Tusita heaven, where he taught the Abhidhamma—the third part of the Pali Canon—to his deceased mother.

Some other issues are problematic in different ways. One of the most controversial episodes in the Canon was the Buddha's decision to admit women into the *sangha*, the monastic community. According to the account in the Vinaya (the second part of the Pali Canon, which includes the rules that monks and nuns are expected to follow), the Buddha was originally reluctant to allow women into the sangha, until his attendant Ananda asked him whether women have the same potential for awakening as men do. The Buddha said yes and then agreed to admit them, provided they submit to some extra rules.

I used to appreciate this incident for the way that the Buddha allowed himself to be persuaded—until I realized that was naïve. There are several textual problems that cast doubt upon the veracity of this story, including an apparent discrepancy between when women were admitted (about five years after the Buddha began to teach) and when Ananda became his attendant (later).

What finally dawned on me, however, is that Ananda's role was probably added later as a way to blame him for the admission of women! There are a number of other incidents in the Pali Canon that seem designed to cast a bad light on him, including a bizarre passage in the Mahaparinibbana Sutta that recounts the last days of the Buddha. In the midst of a straightforward account about his physical decline and death, the Buddha suddenly upbraids Ananda for not noticing the implications of something he'd said a little earlier: due to his well-developed psychic powers, a buddha could actually live many thousands of years, but Ananda didn't catch the hint and ask the Buddha to do so:

> Then, Ananda, the fault is yours. Herein have you failed, inasmuch as you were unable to grasp the plain suggestion, the significant prompting given by the Tathagata, and you did not then entreat the Tathagata to remain. For if you had done so, Ananda, twice the Tathagata might have declined, but the third time he would have consented. Therefore, Ananda, the fault is yours; herein have you failed.

Just in case we miss the point, this ludicrous criticism is repeated twice more. Other accounts strongly suggest that the senior monk Mahakasyapa, who apparently assumed leadership of the sangha after the Buddha's death, had an ongoing quarrel with Ananda, so perhaps it is no coincidence that some other incidents in the Pali Canon seem designed to show Ananda in a bad light.

I mention these magical displays and personal animosities not to belittle the doctrines in the Pali Canon but to question its reliability as historically accurate. The notion that the original events and teachings were transmitted word for word for over three hundred years, without addition or subtraction or "clarification," is implausible to say the least. It is also inconsistent with a significant difference between oral and scriptural traditions. Once there is a written text, whether or not a copy is an exact reproduction becomes more significant and easier to verify. In the oral traditions of nonliterate societies, however, several versions of the most important stories commonly circulate, and there is no single, canonized set of doctrines that practitioners are expected to accept and follow. Without a written text to fixate the words, the emphasis is on conveying the meaning, which allows more liberty of expression. A teacher's own understanding of a topic naturally affects how it is presented, and, inevitably in an oral culture, this sometimes has consequences for how a doctrine is transmitted to future generations.

The customary Theravada emphasis on meticulous memorization and recitation suggests that the Pali Canon might be an exception, but recently discovered Gandharan birch bark scrolls—now the oldest extant Buddhist manuscripts—do not support that possibility. Dating from the first century BCE to the third century CE—the period when the oral teachings probably began to be written down—those scrolls are inconsistent with the traditional belief that a definitive version of what the Buddha said was established during the First Council (presided over by Mahakasyapa) soon after his death. Although they include some familiar material, most of the fragmentary treatises and commentaries reveal new strands of Buddhist literature not included in the Pali Canon as we know it today. Among scholars of early Buddhism, the usual paradigm—that all Buddhist scriptures and schools are branches that diverge from the same tree trunk—has been replaced by a braided river metaphor, with multiple interacting streams that do not derive from a single source. The translator Richard Salomon has summarized the implications: no existing Buddhist collection of early Indian scriptures "can be privileged as the most authentic or original words of the Buddha."

> Nobody holds the view of an original canon anymore.
> —PALI SCHOLAR OSKAR VON HINÜBER

KEEPING IN MIND this nuanced understanding of the Pali Canon, we can return to the issue of what the canon says about nirvana: does it *transcend* this world or is it *immanent* in this world—or is it perhaps something else altogether?

One of the most common descriptions of nirvana is "the end of birth and death": someone who is fully awakened is not born and does not die, as in this well-known passage in the Udana:

> There is, monks, a not-born, a not-brought-to-being, a not-made, a not-formed. If, monks, there were no not-born, not-brought-to-being, not-made, not-formed, no escape would be discerned from what is born, brought-to-being, made, formed. But since there is a not-born, a not-brought-to-being, a not-made, a not-formed, therefore an escape is discerned from what is born, brought-to-being, made, formed.

Another Pali Canon text, the Itivuttaka, contains the same passage and adds some verses that explicitly describe this sublime state as blissful:

> The born, come-to-be, produced,
> The made, the formed, the unlasting,
> Conjoined with decay and death,
> A nest of disease, perishable,

Sprung from nutriment and craving's cord—
That is not fit to take delight in.

The escape from that, the peaceful,
Beyond reasoning, everlasting,
The not-born, the unproduced,
The sorrowless state that is void of stain,
The cessation of states linked to suffering,
The stilling of the conditioned—bliss.

Another Udana passage seems to further distinguish the Buddhist goal from the world we live in now:

Where neither water nor yet earth
Nor fire nor air gain a foothold
There gleam no stars, no sun sheds light.
There shines no moon, yet there no darkness reigns.
When a sage, a brahmin, has come to know this
For himself through his own experience
Then he is freed from form and formlessness
Freed from pleasure and from pain.

Yet a third Udana passage begins in the same way: "There is, monks, that state where there is no earth, no water, no fire, no air..." but goes on to assert that in this state there is "*neither this world nor another world nor both*; neither sun nor moon. Here, monks, I say there is no coming, no going, no staying, no deceasing, no uprising. Not fixed, not movable, it has no support. Just this is the end of suffering" (emphasis mine). Elsewhere we are told that there is no way to measure the consciousness of one who has "gone out," because it is signless, boundless, and all-luminous: *namarupa*, one's name and form, has been destroyed.

EXCEPT PERHAPS for the final Udana quotation, which complicates the issue, such passages seem to support an understanding of nirvana as an unconditioned state or dimension that transcends samsara, which is this world of suffering, craving, and ignorance. The ultimate goal is to escape the unsatisfactory world we now live in by ending physical rebirth. In developing nonattachment, one can come to experience serenity and loving-kindness now, yet they are not in themselves the final solution to dukkha. Although we naturally want to improve our lives while we are here, the main goal is to avoid rebirth, because to be reborn into this world is to suffer.

Nevertheless—and you knew this was coming—there are other important passages in the Pali Canon that seem to offer a more this-worldly interpretation of the ultimate goal. Many Buddhist scholars believe that the Sutta Nipata, in the Khuddaka Nikaya, is part of the oldest stratum of the Canon, so it may provide a better glimpse of the Buddha's original teachings and practices. This becomes especially important when we notice that some of the texts in the Sutta Nipata do not endorse a transcendent solution to dukkha, for they describe awakening as an unselfish, nongrasping way of living here and now.

> In early Buddhism the move from samsara to nirvana is not a journey to a "separate reality," but away from attachment to nonattachment, from greed and anxiety to calm and equanimity, or from "self" to "nonself."
> —DONALD SWEARER

The short Atthakavagga Sutta is a good example. Grace Burford's study of it (*Desire, Death, and Goodness: The Conflict of Ultimate Values in Theravada Buddhism*) emphasizes that the Atthakavagga makes no metaphysical claims about the role of one's *karma* in causing rebirth, or about the importance of escaping the cycle of birth and death. Instead, the sole focus is on overcoming craving and attachment. According to Burford, "It represents simply a transformation of values within human existence," involving *suddhi* purity, *santi* peace, and *panna* wisdom. Because we are addicted to desire, which leads to anxiety and conflict, the solution is just to eliminate that addiction, in which case we can live out the rest of our days serenely and happily.

This view is consistent with some other descriptions of nirvana in the Pali Canon. The goal is often described as simply putting an end to the "three fires" (also known as the "three poisons"): the unwholesome motivations of greed, ill will, and delusion. According to the Samyutta Nikaya, for someone who achieves their destruction, "nirvana is directly visible, immediate, inviting one to come and see, worthy of application, to be personally experienced by the wise."

One of the most interesting descriptions of all is found in the Honeyball Sutta, where the Buddha teaches Bahiya Daruciriya, a wandering ascetic who interrupted the Buddha as he was walking to collect alms. His request for the teachings was so urgent that the Buddha relented and gave him the following pithy response:

> In the seen there is only the seen, in the heard there is only the heard, in the sensed there is only the sensed, in the cognized there is only the cognized: this, Bahiya, is how you should train yourself.
>
> When, Bahiya, there is for you in the seen only the seen, in the heard, only the heard, in the sensed only the sensed, in the cognized only the cognized, then, Bahiya, there is no "you" in connection with that.
>
> When Bahiya, there is no "you" in connection with that, there is no "you" there.
>
> When, Bahiya, there is no "you" there, then, Bahiya, you are neither here nor there nor in between the two.
>
> This, just this, is the end of suffering
>
> —UDANA 1.10

The end of suffering is the most common description of nirvana, which Bahiya attained as soon as he heard these words. We will have occasion to refer to this passage later, but for the moment notice that here too there is no reference to ending rebirth, or attaining some other reality.

It is enough to overcome the sense of a self that is *doing* the seeing, the hearing, and so forth, by focusing on the sights and sounds themselves.

Needless to say, these few references to some passages in the Pali Canon are no substitute for a more thorough analysis of its teachings. They are sufficient, however, to raise doubts about any understanding of nirvana that attempts to find definitive answers in the earliest texts. I have sometimes wondered why the Buddha was not clearer about the nature of nirvana. Was it another way of telling us not to get preoccupied with philosophy? "If you want to understand what nirvana is, experience it yourself!" Yet maybe he was as forthright as he could be. Is the basic problem the limitations of language? Are the discrepancies in the canon because different disciples of the Buddha remembered different discourses or understood them differently? Or did those inconsistencies rise later, due to intentional or inadvertent alteration during oral transmission and explanation? Or are the discrepancies only in our own unawakened minds?

> Half the people in the world think that the metaphors of their religious traditions, for example, are facts. And the other half contends that they are not facts at all. As a result we have people who consider themselves believers because they accept metaphors as facts, and we have others who classify themselves as atheists because they think religious metaphors are lies.
> —JOSEPH CAMPBELL, *Thou Art That: Transforming Religious Metaphor*

My main concern here, however, is to raise questions about any understanding of nirvana as an unconditioned realm distinct from the conditioned world where we live now. One wonders whether such a transcendental interpretation of awakening makes the same mistake that many religious traditions fall into: taking metaphors literally. Realizing the deathless—that which is beyond birth and death—can be understood as attaining another dimension of reality that escapes this impermanent world where everything arises and passes away. It can also be understood as describing what the Buddha recommended to Bahiya: to realize *here and now* that there is no "you" that was ever born or can pass away. In more modern terms, the sense of an "I" that is *having* these experiences is a construct that the Buddha encourages us to deconstruct, because the delusion of a separate self is the source of our most troublesome dukkha. Perhaps that does not involve achieving some other reality but simply reveals the true nature of this one.

The Problem with Transcendence

> The influence of Axial traditions will continue to decline as it becomes ever more apparent that their resources are incommensurate with the moral challenges of the global problematique. In particular, to the extent that these traditions have stressed cosmological dualism and individual salvation we may say they have encouraged an attitude of indifference toward the integrity of natural and social systems.
>
> —LOYAL RUE, *Everybody's Story*

Whether or not the duality between this unsatisfactory world of samsara and some otherworldly goal accurately reflects the original views of the historical Buddha, such dualities are found in many other spiritual traditions that developed around the same time, during what has become known as the *Axial Age* (roughly 800–200 BCE). The German philosopher Karl Jaspers popularized the idea that during this historical period the spiritual foundations of humanity were laid independently in China, India, Persia, Judea, and Greece. In addition to Buddhism, this era gave rise to the Vedanta, Jainism, Confucianism, Taoism, and Judaism, as well as pre-Socratic Greek philosophy and Platonism—which together provide the basis for the most important religious traditions today, including Christianity and Islam.

The Abrahamic faiths discriminate between God the creator (in heaven) and this fallen world. The Vedantic traditions came to differentiate between this deceptive world of *maya* (illusion) and Brahman, the ground of the universe. In both cases, the world as we normally experience it is devalued in comparison with a more transcendent reality. Like these other Axial developments, early Buddhism as usually understood also rests on such a cosmological dualism. Instead of God and his creation, samsara is contrasted with nirvana, with a similar depreciation of this world as a place of suffering, craving, and delusion. And, as with Vedanta and the Abrahamic traditions, the ultimate goal of Buddhist practice has usually been to transcend it. Again, however, we need to ask: what does "transcend it" mean? Escaping to some other reality, or realizing that this world is actually quite different from what we have been believing?

Another aspect of cosmological dualism for these traditions is that *my* individual salvation or personal liberation is independent of yours. As Loyal Rue implies, aspiring to attain a nirvana that transcends this world of samsara may divert us from the ecological and social challenges that confront us right here. Why worry about what's happening now if our ultimate destiny is elsewhere? But if our fundamental dukkha is due to the delusion of a self that feels separate from the rest of the world, then enlightenment should not be understood as that self attaining some other reality. As we will see, another way to understand awakening is that it involves what Dogen describes as "forgetting" oneself—letting go of the sense of self—and realizing one's nonduality with the world. This realization naturally galvanizes a sense of responsibility for the world, because then the well-being of "others" can no longer be detached from one's own.

Despite many differences among the Axial Age traditions, there are remarkable parallels. In general, Axial worldviews were quite distinct from those of previous cultures, such as Mesopotamia and Egypt, which believed that the gods relate to humans mainly through a king, emperor, or pharaoh at the top of the social pyramid. The authority of such rulers was as much sacred as secular, because they were the only ones who had an unmediated relationship with the divine realms; in effect and often in fact, rulers were gods or god-like themselves. In addition to their political responsibilities, they functioned as head priests, conducting rituals

to maintain harmony between the human and the celestial orders—
ceremonies that only they could perform. According to the Egyptologist
Bruce Trigger, the Egyptian pharaoh was "the sole intermediary who
could serve the gods and hence maintain the flows of energy into the
world." The same was true in the Americas: for example, Mayan kings
were "conduits through which supernatural forces were channeled into
the human realm," according to the Maya scholar Lynn Foster.

The activities of these sacred intermediaries were essential for keeping the cosmos in balance. Mesopotamians believed that the gods had
created humans to be their slaves; the cosmic order would be endan-
gered if we did not supply them with food (sacrifices) and homes
(temples). The Aztecs notoriously cut out the still-beating hearts of
sacrificial victims and offered them to the sun god, to keep him on
his course through the heavens; disaster would occur if he veered off
the appointed path. In short, pre-Axial human societies were generally
unfamiliar with a distinction we take for granted today, between religious and secular authority, for they believed that they had an important role to play in maintaining the harmony of the cosmos.

This changed with the Axial revolution, which brought about new
visions of cosmic and moral order, including a new relationship between
the sacred and each individual. In fact, this relationship created the
individual. Instead of relating to the transcendent only through the
mediation of a priest-king, now everyone has his or her own personal
relationship with God, Brahman, or the Tao. In Buddhist terms, each of
us has the same basic nature as the Buddha, which means we have the
same potential to awaken. This also implied a circle of empathy that
included everyone else who has a similar relationship with the sacred.

The most revolutionary aspect of this new relationship was a spiritual demand or expectation that we transform ourselves. It was no
longer enough to fulfill one's social obligations by supporting the ruler's sacrosanct role. Now the Transcendent wanted each individual to
take responsibility for his or her own life. In the Abrahamic traditions
(primarily Judaism, Christianity, Islam) this was first and foremost an
ethical requirement that we live according to God's commandments.

Notice, however, that this impetus to transform comes from something outside this world—which inevitably involves some devaluation of this world. If God is the source of goodness, meaning, and value, the implication seems to be that this world by itself lacks them. And if ending rebirth is the way to end suffering, craving, and delusion, those afflictions must be intrinsic to this world of samsara.

> Praying to an otherworldly God is like kissing through glass.
> —PAUL WEST

In contrast to the ethical focus (good vs. evil) of the Abrahamic faiths, Indian traditions placed more emphasis on a cognitive realization (delusion vs. enlightenment)—a difference that will receive more attention in part III. For example, the Samkhya-Yoga traditions focused on realizing that pure consciousness is distinct from the material world. Brahman, the ground of reality according to the Vedanta traditions, came to be understood as quite different from the particular manifestations or forms experienced in this world. Such metaphysical worldviews also devalue this world. Wise people don't waste their time trying to fix an unreal reality. To awaken is to realize the really Real, which is something other than its appearances.

"Give me a place to stand and I shall move the earth," Archimedes is reputed to have said. Historically, that leverage has been provided by (our belief in) transcendence, which offered the reflective distance—a "higher" perspective—necessary to evaluate and try to change oneself. This also happened politically: the Greeks employed their newly developed philosophical reasoning (another type of transcendence) to assess and restructure their societies, the most famous example being Athenian democracy. To paraphrase what Ernest Renan said about the supernatural, the transcendent is the way in which the *ideal* has made its appearance in human affairs. Because, for example, Martin Luther believed that he was following God's will, he could challenge the enormous authority and power of the Church; so he nailed his ninety-five theses to a church door and declared, "Here I stand. I can do no other." The world we live in today—including our concern for democracy, human rights, and social justice—would be literally unthinkable without the conception of such a superior and supervisory "other world" that developed in the Axial Age.

> Axial Age thinkers...created alternative ideological systems to counteract and protest the empire and politics. They developed moral and legal systems outside the prevailing military and social structures of their day. These systems criticized the status quo and offered an ethical and often religious option rooted in humane values, such as personal responsibility to others, benevolence, virtue, compassion, justice, wisdom, and righteousness. This relativizing of the state and its cults brought human subjectivity and personal morality back into the center of religion.
>
> —RITA NAKASHIMA BROCK AND
> SUSAN BROOKS THISTLETHWAITE

Nevertheless, the conception of another and better world has also been problematic for each of the Axial traditions, including Buddhism. The dualism between the transcendent and this world became reproduced within us, between the "higher" part of ourselves (the soul, rationality) that yearns for escape from this vale of sorrow and the "lower" part that is of the earth (our physical bodies with their emotions and desires). More recent Western versions of this Axial legacy are the mind/body dualism of Rene Descartes, the first modern philosopher, and contemporary "transhumanists" who fantasize about avoiding death by downloading their consciousness into silicon chips.

> For two thousand years man has been living in a dead or dying cosmos, hoping for a heaven hereafter. And all the religions have been religions of the dead body and the postponed reward.
> —D. H. LAWRENCE

The example of transhumanism suggests the problem that encourages us to seek a "higher" reality: as the Buddha emphasized, this world is a place of suffering and death. Much of the attraction of the Axial religions, including Buddhism, is that they seem to offer an escape from mortality. Dread of death also explains our fear and degradation of nature, animals, physical bodies, sex, and women (who bleed and remind us that we are conceived and born like other mammals). We don't want to be of the earth, because we don't want to perish like other animals: we want to be immortal souls that can qualify for heaven. Or nonselves that might attain nirvana! It is no coincidence that all the Axial spiritual traditions, including Buddhism, have also been patriarchal: the hierarchy between higher and lower worlds became reproduced in the hierarchy of men over women.

> The male body becomes an instrument of dominance
> and control.... The female body becomes a symbol
> on which men project and act out a series of ideas
> about sexuality, birth, physical existence, and intimacy.
> —BROCK AND THISTLEWAITE

One is reminded of the inferior status of women that became institutionalized in every Abrahamic tradition, although Buddhists are hardly in a position to throw stones. Despite passages in the Pali Canon that express repulsion for women's bodies, other stories suggest that in this regard too the historical Buddha was more liberated than the organizations that developed to preserve and follow his teachings. The subordinate status of ordained women in Buddhist societies, and institutional resistance against restoring full ordination for women in almost every Asian society (Taiwan being the notable exception), shows that patriarchy remains a deeply- engrained problem for traditional Buddhist cultures.

That each person now had a personal relationship with transcendence had democratic implications, but with few exceptions (such as briefly and incompletely in ancient Athens) those possibilities would not be developed until modernity. In the meantime, the hierarchical relationship between a higher reality and the human world also provided a model for reproducing and justifying inequitable social structures. According to Brock and Thistlewaite, Axial Age religions "were often metaphorically and mythically appropriated to structure power within their own systems. Hierarchical images of totalitarian power were transmuted into benevolent images."

Today we are increasingly challenged by another hierarchy of domination and privilege, that between *Homo sapiens sapiens* and the (rest of the) natural world. The Axial dualism between higher and lower worlds has become replicated in the alienation between the collective ego (or "wego") of humanity and the rest of the biosphere, which is suffering the consequences of our institutionalized greed and exploitation. Rapid climate change—no longer just a future possibility—calls upon us to achieve a new relationship that acknowledges our nonduality with the earth and responsibility to the earth, which is not just our home but our mother. Part III will consider the striking parallels between our perennial individual predicament—the delusive sense of a self that is separate from others—and our collective predicament today in relation to the biosphere.

To these three axiological critiques of cosmological dualism— oppressive hierarchies of men over women, rulers over ruled, and humanity over the rest of the natural world—must be added the critical perspective provided by the physical sciences, whose explanatory success constitutes the greatest challenge to any religious belief in a world that transcends this one. Today the biggest problem with such dualisms is, of course, that the most reputable source of knowledge in the modern world has not discovered anything that supports them. God used to live in a heaven above the clouds, but now we have a different understanding of what exists above and beyond the earth's atmosphere.

Taken together, these evaluations do not refute the possibility of a dimension of reality that transcends this world, but they encourage us to interrogate this way of conceptualizing the Buddhist experience of awakening. It becomes difficult to avoid the conclusion that, although Axial-type transcendence has been historically invaluable, it is no longer adequate for what we know today. Such conceptions provided the symbolic leverage that freed us from the embeddedness of pre-Axial societies, but today we need to be liberated from their dualisms, which have outlived their role. Is there another paradigm that might offer the transformative leverage we still need, without devaluing this world?

The Problem with Immanence

> One does not become enlightened by imagining figures of light, but by making the darkness conscious.
>
> —CARL JUNG

Partly in reaction to the cosmological dualism between samsara and nirvana, a this-worldly alternative has become popular in modern Buddhism, especially in the West: understanding the Buddhist path as a program of psychological development that helps us cope with personal problems, especially one's "monkey mind" and its afflictive emotions.

Whenever Buddhism has spread to another culture, it has interacted with the belief systems of that culture, resulting in the development of something new. Today the main site of interaction within the West is not Judeo-Christianity but psychology, a relationship that has led to innovative types of psychotherapy and, most recently, to the extraordinary success of the mindfulness movement.

There is already a large and rapidly growing literature on the relationship between Buddhism and psychotherapy. Many Western-trained psychotherapists have become Buddhist practitioners and incorporate contemplative techniques into their therapy; some of them have also become authorized as Buddhist teachers. Buddhism is providing new perspectives on the nature of psychological well-being and new practices that help to promote it.

There are a host of problems that individuals have that Buddhism was never designed to address, including the whole spectrum of mental

illness, from anxiety to depression to psychosis,
and to the nuts and bolts of couples' issues.

—Harvey Aronson

On the other side, more than a generation of Buddhist practice by committed Western students has made it apparent that meditation by itself is sometimes insufficient to resolve deep-rooted psychological problems and relationship difficulties. In its own short history the psychotherapeutic tradition has gained considerable insight into the mechanisms of denial, rationalization, repression, projection, and so forth, which can help us understand how Buddhist practice sometimes goes wrong—for example, the complicated transference/countertransference that can distort the relationship between therapist and client (or between teacher and disciple).

Transference, as originally defined by psychoanalysts, is the unconscious tendency of a patient to take emotions and behavioral patterns felt toward one person (for example, a parent) and transfer them to another (one's psychoanalyst or guru). Countertransference occurs when the analyst (or teacher) also gets caught up in that transference. If a spiritual teacher is surrounded by a coterie of devotees who look upon him or her as god-like, that is transference. When that teacher begins to agree with them, that is countertransference—in Buddhist terms, a delusion incompatible with our usual understanding of awakening, yet not uncommon.

Traditional Buddhist teachings do not identify such mechanisms because the focus has been different. In Mahayana terms, Buddhist practice emphasizes realizing the "emptiness" of psychological phenomena, while psychotherapy emphasizes understanding how they affect our relationships, including one's relationship with oneself. The important discovery is that the two approaches can supplement each other because they share the same basic concern: alleviating our suffering.

Clients begin their journey in psychotherapy with similar intentions to the ones Buddha had when he set out on his

spiritual journey. What is the truth about my life? Who am I
and why do I do things the way I do? Why am I still unhappy
when I have everything? Therapy is all about getting real.
We begin close to home assessing the current state of affairs
of our life and relationships. We start with our neurotic self
and look at the ways we try to get personal freedom, love,
and connection, but only suffer and come up empty handed.
Similar to when we begin meditation, we can only start from
where we are.

—TINA FOSSELLA

The main challenge for each side in this dialogue is resisting the
temptation to swallow the other. It's easy for a therapist to reject Buddhist awakening as an escapist fantasy and just as easy for Buddhists
to dismiss a psychotherapeutic focus on relationship problems as
obsessing with past events rather than living fully in the present. This
temptation is aggravated by the fact that the cultural and historical
gap between them is so great, which tends to activate our Eurocentrism (which psychotherapist and long-time meditator Jeffrey Rubin
defines as "the intellectually imperialistic tendency in much Western
scholarship to assume that European and North American standards
and values are the center of the moral and intellectual universe") or
to idealize Orientocentrism ("the idealizing and privileging of Asian
thought—treating it as sacred—and the neglect if not dismissal of the
value of Western psychological perspectives"). If we are honest with
ourselves, most of us have a bias that favors one side or the other.

It's not easy to steer a course between them, and that's the challenge:
together they can help to free us from seeking a security of sorts by identifying with one particular way of thinking, such as the categories of
Freudian psychoanalysis or the paradoxes of Chan/Zen. Rubin describes
this pitfall in *Psychotherapy and Buddhism: Toward an Integration*:

Fitting in with the institutional ethos, including minimizing
self-vulnerability, enables trainees to solidify their precari-

ous status. Embracing the theories of the school to which one identifies offers a sense of intellectual and emotional comfort.... It also gives one a stable identity and sense of belonging. But it fosters unrealistic ideals and expectations of self-knowledge, self-mastery, and selfless service, as well as a phobic stance toward emotional distress and vulnerability. Psychotherapists may thus have great difficulty acknowledging or coping with their own vulnerability.

For *trainee psychotherapists* substitute *Buddhist practitioners* and the passage offers as much insight into where Buddhists can get stuck.

Dwelling "in-between"—what might be called *the position of no fixed position*—does not mean rejecting either perspective but being able to appreciate both. Each is realized to be a heuristic construct that can be helpful, according to the situation, yet neither has exclusive claims to the Truth. This extends a hard-won psychotherapeutic insight into the relativity of its own divergent schools and perspectives. Irvin Yalom puts it well:

> Therapists may offer the patient any number of explanations to clarify the same issue.... *None, despite vehement claims to the contrary, has sole rights to the truth.* After all, they are all based on imaginary "as if" structures.... They are all fictions, psychological constructs created for semantic convenience, and they justify their existence only by virtue of their explanatory power.

We need such fictions because our minds do not function in a vacuum but are activated by their constructs. The Buddha was also careful not to set up his teachings as the only truth; in the Canki Sutta he says, "It is not proper for a wise man...to come to the conclusion 'this alone is truth, and everything else is false.'" He compared his teachings to a raft that can be used to ferry ourselves across the river of suffering to the "other shore" of enlightenment—and then to be abandoned, not carried around on one's back. If psychotherapeutic explanations are all imaginary "as if" structures justified by the ways they help us change, and if Buddhist truths are fingers not to be confused with the moon they point at—or, to use a better metaphor, if they are roadmaps showing us the way to go—then the door opens for a genuine cross-cultural inquiry with profound implications for how we understand and transform ourselves.

That door may be open, yet it's also important not to minimize the challenges involved in a dialogue between two such very different approaches. Harvey Aronson pinpoints some of them in his important book *Buddhist Practice on Western Ground: Reconciling Eastern Ideals and Western Psychology*:

> Buddhist teachers counsel us to abandon anger, develop patience, give up attachment, and understand the absence of self; this is taught in a context of disciplined communal practice—the sangha. Therapists, conversely, encourage those who are emotionally shut down to experience feelings of anger, and they facilitate the quest for relationship and intimacy; this is done in a context that supports self-assertion and individuality. How are we to follow both approaches?

The disparities that Aronson lists constellate around one basic difference: traditional psychotherapeutic approaches are concerned to help *heal* the self, whereas the Buddhist model of well-being emphasizes liberating insight into the *delusion* of self and developing what Rubin terms "non-self-centric subjectivity." Rubin argues that neither tradition by itself provides the full picture of who we are, what our problem is, and how we transform. In *Psychotherapy and Buddhism*, he argues, "For example, Buddhist models of health could teach psychoanalysis that there are possibilities for emotional well-being that far exceed the limits described by psychoanalytic models, while psychoanalysis could help Buddhism understand some of the unconscious interferences to meditation practice and the growth practice."

The good news is that the burgeoning field of Buddhist (and other types of transpersonal) psychotherapy is aware of the difference and has begun to explore the relationship between the two. Buddhism emphasizes nonattachment: when a thought or emotion arises during meditation, we are encouraged to let it go. Yet one of the most important psychoanalytic discoveries since Freud has been realizing the vital role of healthy attachment in early life.

> There is a whole body of study and research in Western psychology showing how close bonding and loving attunement—what is known as "secure attachment"—have powerful impacts on every aspect of human development. Secure attachment has a tremendous effect on many dimensions of our health, wellbeing, and capacity to function effectively in the world: how our brains form, how well our endocrine and immune systems function, how we handle emotions, how subject we are to depression, how our nervous system functions and handles stress, and how we relate to others. Modern culture and child raising leave most people suffering from symptoms of insecure attachment: self-hatred, disembodiment, lack of grounding, ongoing insecurity and anxiety, overactive minds, inability to deeply trust, and a deep sense of inner deficiency. So most of us suffer from an extreme degree of alienation and disconnection that was unknown in earlier times—from society, community, family, older generations, nature, religion, tradition, our body, our feelings, and our humanity itself.
>
> —JOHN WELWOOD

So how does one reconcile the Buddhist ideal of nonattachment with the importance of human attachment in childhood development? Welwood is worth quoting again because he explains it so well:

In terms of human evolution, nonattachment is an advanced

teaching. I'm suggesting that we need to be able to form satisfying human attachments before genuine nonattachment is possible. Otherwise, someone suffering from insecure attachment is likely to confuse nonattachment with avoidant attachment behavior. For avoidant types, attachment is actually threatening and scary. So healing for avoidant types would involve becoming willing and able to feel their needs for human connectedness, instead of spiritually bypassing them. Once that happens, then nonattachment starts to make some sense.

Welwood uses the term *spiritual bypassing* to refer to the way that spiritual practices can be used to avoid feelings and other psychological issues: "being a 'good' spiritual practitioner can become a *compensatory identity* that covers up and defends against an underlying *deficient identity*, where we feel bad about ourselves, not good enough, or basically lacking. Then, although we may be practicing diligently, our spiritual practice can be used in the service of denial and defense." Jack Engler, a psychotherapist and meditation teacher who is one of the pioneers of transpersonal psychology, offers some examples: "Teachings on no-self can be used to rationalize a lack of integration or cohesive self; teachings on nonattachment can rationalize an inability to form relationships; enlightenment can be used as some type of idealized grandiose self; and devotion to a teacher can allow one to feel special in mirroring the idealized other and masking internal feelings of inferiority."

We can be hopeful about the future of this dialogue because it is anchored empirically in what really works to reduce the dukkha of therapeutic patients and Buddhist practitioners. Given the premodern roots of the Buddhist tradition, the question from a psychotherapeutic perspective is whether Buddhist teachings mythologize the developmental process by understanding the ultimate goal as transcending this world of suffering and delusion. Given the secular roots and pragmatic goals of psychotherapy, the question from a Buddhist perspective is whether such therapies still retain too limited an understanding of our human potential, ignoring possibilities that transcend modern assumptions about what it means to be human.

The tension between these two questions is what makes the conversation between the two perspectives so fascinating. That tension has largely been absent in the extraordinary success of the mindfulness movement.

> Absence of psychoneurotic illness may be health, but
> it is not life.... We are poor indeed if we are only sane.
> —Donald Winnicott

Mindfulness

Suddenly the mindfulness movement has become mainstream, making its way into schools, corporations, prisons, and government agencies including the military. The media now regularly cite scientific studies that report on the numerous health benefits of mindfulness meditation and how such a simple practice can effect significant neurological changes in the brain.

These are beneficial and promising developments—yet they have a shadow, perhaps most evident in some of the ways that corporate cultures have embraced the practice. Some Buddhists have celebrated the success of the mindfulness movement as the "Trojan horse" that is helping Buddhism to infiltrate and transform modern society, but if that metaphor is apt it is not yet clear which is the horse and which is Troy.

> Mindfulness means paying attention in a particular way:
> on purpose, in the present moment, and nonjudgmentally.
> —John Kabat-Zinn

Proponents of mindfulness training often ignore or de-emphasize its Buddhist roots (though there can be a certain cachet in branding their programs as "Buddhist-inspired"). Uncoupling mindfulness from its ethical and religious context is understandable as an expedient move to make such training a viable product in the marketplace of self-help methodologies. While a stripped-down, secularized approach—sometimes disparaged as "McMindfulness"—often makes it more palatable to the business world, decontextualizing mindfulness from its original liberative and transformative purpose, including its foundation in social ethics, can lose sight of why it is so important. Rather than mindfulness as a means to awaken individuals and organizations from the "three poisons" that the Buddha identified—the unwholesome roots of greed, ill will, and delusion—it is sometimes refashioned into a technique that can indirectly reinforce those roots.

Most scientific and popular accounts circulating in the media portray mindfulness in terms of stress reduction and attention-enhancement, yet mindfulness, as understood and practiced within the Buddhist tradition, is not merely an ethically neutral practice for reducing stress and improving concentration. Rather, it is a *distinct quality of attention* that depends upon many other factors: the nature of one's thoughts, speech, and actions; one's way of making a living; and one's efforts to avoid unwholesome and unskillful behaviors, while developing those that are conducive to wise action, social harmony, and compassion. For Buddhism the practice of mindfulness is an integral part of the ultimate goal, which involves seeing through the delusion of a separate self and learning to live in a way that is consistent with such a realization.

The crucial issue is whether the quality of one's awareness is characterized by wholesome intentions and positive mental qualities that lead to human flourishing and a concern for the well-being of others, as well as for oneself. The mindful attention and single-minded concentration of a terrorist or criminal is not the right mindfulness (*sama-sati*, the seventh factor on the Eightfold Path) that the Dalai Lama has developed.

In the business world, mindfulness meditation is often marketed as a method for personal self-fulfillment, a reprieve from the ordeals of corporate life. Although such an individualistic and consumer orientation to the practice may be effective for self-preservation and self-advancement, it is essentially impotent for mitigating the causes of collective and organizational dukkha. After a mindfulness program, individual employees in a company may feel that their stress, unhappiness, and doubts are entirely self-made. Such training promotes a tacit acceptance of the status quo and becomes an instrumental tool for keeping attention focused on institutional goals. When mindfulness practice is compartmentalized in this way, however, there is a disconnection between one's own personal transformation and the kind of organizational restructuring that might address the causes and conditions of suffering in the broader environment. Such a colonization of mindfulness reorients the practice to the needs of the company, rather than encouraging a critical reflection on the causes of our collective suffering, or *social dukkha*. Bhikkhu Bodhi, one of the foremost American Buddhist monastics, has warned: "absent a sharp social critique, Buddhist practices could easily be used to justify and stabilize the status quo, becoming a reinforcement of consumer capitalism."

According to the American Institute of Stress, "companies lose an estimated $300 billion annually to lowered productivity, absenteeism, health care, and related costs stemming from stress." So far, however, the mindfulness movement has avoided any serious consideration of why stress is so pervasive in modern business institutions. The *New York Times* has described Google's mindfulness program as "sort of an organizational WD-40, a necessary lubricant between driven, ambitious employees and Google's demanding corporate culture." Cloaked in an aura of care and humanity, mindfulness can be refashioned into a safety valve, as a way to let off steam—a technique for coping with the anxieties and tensions of corporate life.

Jeremy Carrette and Richard King, in their book *Selling Spirituality: The Silent Takeover of Religion*, argue that the business world "exploits the transformative power of traditional 'spiritual disciplines' by reorienting their fundamental goals. Instead of the more traditional emphasis upon self-sacrifice, the disciplining of desire, and a recognition of community, we find productivity, work-efficiency, and the accumulation of profit put forward as the new goals."

> When we quit thinking primarily about ourselves
> and our own self-preservation, we undergo
> a truly heroic transformation of consciousness.
> —JOSEPH CAMPBELL

The basic problem with such an instrumentalist approach to mindfulness practice is that it tends to subvert the most important goal of the Buddhist path. If the ultimate source of my dukkha is the delusion of self, the solution to that dukkha involves realizing that I am not really separate from other people and therefore should not pursue my own well-being with indifference to theirs. Then using mindfulness to make an individual or an organization more efficient and productive can address superficial types of dukkha while reinforcing its deepest, most problematic form: the inherent anxiety of a deluded self that feels disconnected from others. The context is important: "paying attention nonjudgmentally" can end up rationalizing a very problematic environment. Accepting and adapting to the way things are is often wise, but not always.

THIS IS NOT A CRITIQUE of the mindfulness movement itself but of the ways it is sometimes misappropriated, and of the hype sometimes used to promote it. It goes without saying that in the business world too mindfulness programs can be of enormous benefit to those who take them. There is even some evidence that mindfulness practice tends to make practitioners more empathic and compassionate, regardless of one's initial motivations. If that finding continues to be empirically substantiated, it would have great implications. And the value of mindfulness training in the medical and educational fields is rightly celebrated, including its success with military veterans who suffer from PTSD.

Nevertheless, these positive benefits do not allow us to sidestep the basic issue: is a watered-down version of a profoundly transformative spiritual path becoming widely acceptable because it helps us adapt to some of the questionable values of contemporary society?

Or does mindfulness practice encourage us to evaluate our collective situation from a more Buddhist perspective? Arguably, the three poisons of greed, aggression, and delusion are not only rampant individually but have become institutionalized in our economic system, in our militarism, and in the corporate media that normalize their abuses. Should such institutionalized poisons be taken for granted, as just the way things are, or challenged as incompatible with Buddhist principles?

This leads to other questions about the motivations and social implications of Buddhist practice. We come to Buddhism because we suffer, one way or another. Almost inevitably, then, at the beginning of our practice we are preoccupied with what we need to do to deal with that personal suffering. If the ultimate problem is the delusion of self, there can be some irony in this self-preoccupation, yet it is usually necessary, at least at the beginning. The issue is whether we remain stuck there indefinitely—an attitude that our individualistic, self-absorbed culture encourages—or whether we eventually realize that pursuing our own well-being cannot be sharply distinguished from promoting the well-being of others.

> When we feel compassion for others,
> we naturally have a sense of our own value.
> —HARVEY ARONSON

A recent critique of contemporary Buddhism by the influential philosopher Slavoj Zizek addresses this issue squarely. In his view, Western Buddhism is becoming "the hegemonic ideology of global capitalism" because its "meditative stance is arguably the most efficient way for us to fully participate in capitalist dynamics while retaining the appearance of mental sanity." Western Buddhism "enables you to fully participate in the frantic pace of the capitalist game while sustaining the perception that you are not really in it; that you are well aware of how worthless this spectacle is; and that what really matters to you is the peace of the inner Self to which you know you can always withdraw."

Some of his language suggests that Zizek does not know much about Buddhist teachings, but he is a perceptive observer of contemporary culture, and he notices a role that Buddhism is serving within that culture. Will that become Buddhism's primary role? Will Buddhism become "secularized, detraditionalized, and oriented exclusively toward the individual" in the same way that yoga has, according to Carrette and King?

I have focused on the corporate appropriation of mindfulness practice because it is a good example of what I am calling an *immanentist* approach (in contrast to the *transcendentalist* approach discussed earlier). If traditional Asian versions of Buddhism include a premodern acceptance of cosmological dualism, then understanding mindfulness practice as the "essence" of Buddhism normally takes for granted a secular worldview—which does not usually allow for the possibility of an awakening that challenges that understanding. Both attitudes preclude a more interesting opportunity: a genuine conversation between traditional Buddhism and secular modernity that does not assume the validity of either paradigm but puts both into question, as each interrogates the other.

In a curious way, transcendent views of awakening and immanent views of practice can fit together quite comfortably, even reinforce each other. If my ultimate goal is something or somewhere else, I don't need to be too concerned about what's happening here and now. And if the goal of my practice is to de-stress so I can perform my usual work and home roles better, I won't be inclined to consider the larger social and ecological implications of the Buddhist perspective. In both cases, the radical nature of the Buddhist critique of self is unappreciated, and the new possibilities that arise when we realize our nonduality with this world remain unfulfilled.

Beyond Transcendence and Immanence

Buddhism as psychological therapy or mindfulness practice tends to underemphasize the traditional role of moral precepts, community practice, and especially enlightenment, which has always been understood as something more deeply transformative than simply helping one adjust to the stresses of daily life. If transcendence encourages disidentifying from our lives here, because it is focused on *escaping this world*, the mindfulness movement and some other psychotherapeutic appropriations of Buddhism tend to *accept this world as it is*—or, more precisely, to presuppose the prevalent, Western-derived worldview about who we are, what the world really is, and our role within it. But what if that understanding of reality is one of the main causes of our dukkha?

Rather than devaluing this world by trying to end rebirth into it, or attempting to make the best of our lives within it as it is (or as it seems to be), there is a third possibility: we can "wake up" by realizing something usually unnoticed about the nature of this world, right here and now, and integrate that realization into our daily lives.

The Buddha warned against *eternalism* and *annihilationism*. Eternalism is the view that the self survives death. Annihilationism is the opposite view, that the self is destroyed at death. Both beliefs suffer from the same misconception: that there is a discrete self, which either is destroyed or is not destroyed when the body dies. They assume the same duality between a self and the world it is "in."

Much the same is true for the two solutions to dukkha discussed above. With the transcendentalist approach I want to escape this unsatisfactory world, but what is this "I" that wants to go somewhere else? Instead of focusing on a practice that can clarify the nature of the "I"—that can help overcome my sense of separation from others—I seek an individual solution that is immune to what is happening to the rest of the world. Although the alternative psychological approach is this-worldly, it also tends to assume the usual understanding of ourselves as separate individuals with separate lives in a world where one should make the best of one's dwindling time—but without any hope of evading our inevitable and dreadful fate.

Do both miss the point? Buddhist enlightenment is not simply a more mindful adaptation to our unfortunate existential condition, nor is it attaining some other dimension that is distinct from and therefore indifferent to this world. Rather, it is a transformative realization that the world as we usually experience it (including the way that I usually experience myself) is neither real nor unreal but a *psychological and social construction* that can be deconstructed and reconstructed, which is what happens when one follows the Buddhist path.

> Whatever we call reality, it is revealed to us only through an active construction in which we participate.
> —NOBEL LAUREATE ILYA PRIGOGINE

Not until the German philosopher Immanuel Kant in the late eighteenth century did the West begin to realize that what we normally take to be the real world is a construction. According to Kant the mind does not simply receive sense-impressions from the outside; using its own innate categories—which include time, space, and causality—it organizes those sense-impressions into the world we are familiar with. Because this happens preconsciously, we usually take the result for granted, as "just the way things are."

Kant realized something else about this process: what is normally experienced as myself—my sense of being a self that perceives, thinks, feels, and acts—does not do this constructing. Rather, "I" am one of the *results* of this construction, along with the world that I suppose to be external to me. For spiritual traditions such as Buddhism this has very important implications: the subjective sense of a self *inside* that is separate from an objective reality *outside* is a product of the ways that our minds usually function.

Because we ordinarily experience only the consequences of this unconscious process, Kant realized that we do not know what "the world-in-itself" is really like, nor the true nature of the self. Although he was not completely clear on this point, Kant did not allow for the possibility of a deconstruction that would lead to experiencing either of them directly, since all of our conscious experience is already conditioned by the construction process. This is where Buddhism provides a different perspective and offers a different possibility.

Examining Buddhist texts from a constructivist viewpoint sheds considerable light on the traditional teachings. The Pali Canon, in particular, abounds in references to how the mind "fabricates" what we usually take to be reality. The five *khanda* (*skandha* in Sanskrit) are literally "heaps"—of forms, sensations, perceptions, mental dispositions (*sankhara*), and consciousness—whose interaction composes the sense of self. Again, not a real self, but the illusion of a separate self. And *paticcasamuppada* (*pratitya-samutpada* in Sanskrit) or "conditioned arising"—often considered the single most important doctrine in early Buddhism—explains in detail how our delusions and cravings work together to construct the way we experience the world.

Let's try a more modern way to describe the problem with this construction, followed by the deconstruction that Buddhist practice involves.

Constructing the Self and Its World

Looking around the room where I am writing these words, I see many different objects: pens, papers, paper clips, reproductions of some paintings on the walls...you get the idea. Actually, though, seeing the room in this way is not that simple, because it involves a couple different processes: my eyes perceiving colored shapes, and my mind identifying them with a name: *that* is a pen. Moreover, there's a third process involved. I don't see a bunch of objects that just happen to be where they are. Instead, to see something *as* a pen is to also "see" its function, which is implied by its name: the pen is for writing with, the sheets of paper can be written on, and so forth. So, when I'm looking around the room, what I normally notice is not material things but functional *possibilities*.

> The mistake is to suppose that the application of language
> to the world consists of attaching labels to objects
> that are, so to speak, self-identifying. On my view,
> the world divides the way we divide it, and our main way
> of dividing things up is in language.
> —JOHN SEARLE

We are not usually aware of the differences between these three aspects of the seeing process, but the Buddhist tradition emphasizes them, because they are not always as innocuous as my examples. They explain how craving works and also imply how we can free ourselves from it.

Although different Buddhist thinkers have divided up perception into different phases, fundamentally they agree about the nature of the process. The Mahayana scholar Edward Conze summarized it into three stages: (1) an object of attention provides (2) a basis for recognition, which then becomes (3) an occasion for what he calls "entrancement." In the first stage, awareness turns toward a "bare" percept, such as a colored shape. In the second stage, that colored shape is recognized as, for example, a bar of chocolate. Once the shape is identified, predispositions get activated in the third stage. Someone who loves chocolate (bittersweet, please) will tend to respond in conditioned and predictable ways.

This whole sequence normally occurs so quickly that we take it to be one simple event: "being attracted to a bar of chocolate." But that enticing bar is actually the product of a three-part mental construction that, contrary to what Kant may have believed, can be deconstructed. Buddhism emphasizes that meditative practice can teach us to distinguish the separate stages; in fact, to experience that first stage by itself is an important goal of the Buddhist path, because it frees us from the automatized craving that leads to automatized responses that lead to dukkha.

> The task is to bring the process back to the initial point,
> before any "superimpositions" have distorted
> the actual and initial datum.
> —EDWARD CONZE

Yet there's more to it than that—and this is where it gets really interesting. What did the Buddha say to Bahiya in the Honeyball Sutta? "When there is for you in the seen only the seen, in the heard only the heard, in the sensed only the sensed, in the cognized only the cognized, then, Bahiya, there is no 'you' in connection with that.... When there is no 'you' there, then you are neither here nor there nor in between the two. This, just this, is the end of suffering."

The Buddha is saying, in effect, that distinguishing the initial stage of just-seeing deconstructs not only the supposed *object* of craving but also the supposed *subject* who craves. That's because the original process of "putting together" the three stages, which results in "entrancement," is what also creates the illusion of a self that is entranced. The basic problem isn't just that I *crave* and can never get enough of what's craved. It's that *I* crave: that craving involves the illusion of a craver, who by definition can never be satisfied, as we'll see.

In this way our experience polarizes into an external world that one is aware *of* and the internal sense of an "I" that *has* that awareness. The act of grasping creates the illusory subject-object distinction between that-which-is-grasped and that-which-grasps. It is the (constructed) duality between them that's the root ignorance and cause of the fundamental dukkha at the core of the human condition.

Needless to say, there's something counterintuitive about this claim. There's no *me*? I can doubt that what I experience is real—"maybe it's only a dream"—but how can I doubt that *I* am the one having the experience? Didn't Descartes jump-start modern philosophy by arguing "I think, therefore I am"?

He did, and much of twentieth-century philosophy was devoted to showing his mistake. His argument isn't valid: the notion that *he* was *doing* the thinking is really an unwarranted addition to the actual experience, which in itself was simpler: just *thinking*. In fact, that's often the first thing we learn when we begin to meditate. We come to meditation with the usual assumption that the thoughts and images and feelings that arise are *something that I am doing*, only to realize that the thoughts, etc.. have a life of their own. It's more correct to say that *the thoughts are "doing" me*: that my sense of self is composed of mostly habitual ways of thinking, feeling, acting, reacting, remembering, planning, intending, and so forth. They usually determine what "I" think, say, and do. In that sense, free will isn't something we all have as a birthright, but something that can be developed. Another word for Buddhist enlightenment is *liberation*: freedom from the delusion of self, and from the conditioned tendencies that largely compose it.

> A great many people think they are thinking
> when they are merely rearranging their prejudices.
> —WILLIAM JAMES

A traditional contemplative practice involves looking for the "I" that is supposedly having or doing all these processes, as with the Zen koan: "*Who* is hearing that sound?" There is awareness of sound, but the nature of that awareness is what needs to be clarified. One's thinking, feeling, intending, etc.. constantly relate back to the self-image of a "me," yet that image too is a conditioned construct.

Conditioned by what? By earlier experiences, both passive (what happened to "me") and active (what "I" did in response). Traditional Buddhist teachings trace one's sankhara tendencies back to earlier lifetimes, and modern psychologists back to early childhood development. Babies aren't born with a sense of self. That develops over time, usually according to a sequence of developmental stages that have been well-studied, and an important aspect of that development is interaction with caregivers. The growing child *internalizes* a sense of self by learning to communicate with others who already have a sense of self, such as Mom. A baby without a human caregiver, such as an abandoned child adopted by wolves, will never become fully human unless it is recovered soon, because to be human is as much a social as a biological accomplishment.

As this implies, to develop a sense of self is healthy and necessary. According to Buddhism, the problem isn't that we have a self; on the contrary, there's never been a real self, so there's nothing to discard. Nor do we need to get rid of the sense of self; that's necessary to function in daily life. The problem is a sense of self that feels and believes itself to be *separate* from the rest of the world. What's important to realize is that (as Mahayana puts it) the sense of self is "empty" of any self-existence.

Realizing that the sense of self is a construct gives us insight into why it is the source of our most problematic dukkha. A constructed self is not something that has any discrete reality of its own. It's a cluster of impermanent and interacting psycho-physical processes that are not grounded in anything more substantial. It is ungrounded because a cluster of always-changing processes is ungroundable. It is insecure because there's nothing there that ever could be secured.

That sounds uncomfortable, to say the least, yet being ungroundable is actually not the problem. The problem is the conscious or unconscious understanding that I, as a being separate from others and from the rest of the world, *need* to secure myself somehow—a project doomed never to succeed.

Elsewhere I've described this situation by saying that the sense of (separate) self is shadowed or haunted by a sense of *lack*—the feeling that something is wrong with me, or that something is missing in my life. This points to one of the great secrets of life: each of us has this sense of lack, but we are not usually aware that everyone else feels it too.

There's an irony here. The problem, again, is not that each of us feels this basic lack, but that we don't know why we have it—that we don't understand where the sense of lack comes from. Properly understood, the sense of lack is what motivates us to undertake the spiritual path, which is what's necessary to really resolve it. Yet what usually happens is that the problem becomes projected and therefore insoluble: I believe that what I lack is something outside myself, so I become preoccupied with external things.

Is a sense of lack inherent to the human condition? The Genesis story of Adam and Eve, and their expulsion from the Garden of Eden, is presented in the Bible as an act of disobedience and punishment, yet it makes more sense to me as a fable about the consequences of self-awareness, which is what induces them to don fig leaves and hide from God. If so, the original problem isn't sin but our sense of lack, which is the shadow that usually dogs our self-consciousness.

This myth is also an "origin story" that explains how civilization began—and perhaps even how religion began. Have religious beliefs and practices been humankind's traditional way of trying to cope with the sense of lack? We respond to our feelings of lack and disconnection by conducting rituals and offering sacrifices, to get back into the good graces of the gods and harmonize with the cosmic powers. Then we feel better—for a while.

In order for any society to function successfully, it must offer ways for its members to deal with their sense of lack. Another way to say this is that every social system provides an explanation for it and conditions its members to respond to it in acceptable ways. A peasant living in Europe a thousand years ago soon learned the cause of her sense of lack: sin. She inherited the original sin of Adam and Eve, in addition to her own sins, and the Church offered collective, socially maintained ways to cope with it. If you attend mass, confess your sins, perform penance, and so forth, then there is a good chance that you will go to heaven after you die, where your lack will disappear as you join the company of angels...

But what if you live in a more secular society, where traditional religious explanations are no longer convincing for many people? In that case your sense of lack may be even stronger, because your sense of being a separate individual is stronger. Then a sense of something lacking is your own personal problem, and you must find your own way to (try to) fill up your sense of lack and become more grounded and substantial.

This gives us insight into why our culture is so obsessed with money, fame, and romance—three of our most popular "reality projects," as I describe them in *Money Sex War Karma*. We usually think of our pre-occupation with money, for example, as indicating how materialistic our society has become, yet in itself money (whether paper bills or digits in bank accounts) is worthless; it's a social symbol that has value only because a collective agreement (legally enforced) makes it the medium of exchange—which makes money *pure value*, in effect. Inevitably, however, our sense of lack affects its symbolic value: since money represents the possibility of obtaining almost anything we want, and since obtaining whatever we want is what we usually think will make us happy, money comes to symbolize happiness.

I won't repeat any more of that discussion here, except to reiterate the basic defect with such obsessions: since they are only symptoms of the actual problem, rather than the problem itself, they are unable to resolve one's sense of lack. No matter how much money you may accumulate, or how famous you may become, it won't ever be enough for the self to feel secure in its delusive separateness. That brings us back to the path that can deconstruct one's sense of lack, by deconstructing the sense of self it shadows.

Nonattachment

The solution to our festering sense of lack is deconstructing and reconstructing the sense of self, so that it doesn't feel so separate. The Buddha's response to Bahiya points the way: by focusing on "just the seen," the three-stage sequence that creates the sense of a partition between seer and seen, between self inside and the external world, can be undone.

The Buddhist path includes a variety of practices, including ethical precepts, contemplative exercises, and wisdom teachings, to deconstruct that delusive duality. Ironically, given the goal of feeling less "separate," the most important practice is nonattachment—Welwood's "advanced teaching"—which is necessary to realize the true nature of one's mind, which has no fixed form of its own. The Astasahasrika Sutra, one of the most important texts in the Mahayana tradition, begins by going right to the heart of this issue:

> No wisdom can we get hold of, no highest perfection,
> No bodhisattva, no thought of enlightenment either.
> When told of this, if not bewildered and in no way anxious,
> A bodhisattva courses in the Tathagata's wisdom.
> In form, in feeling, will, perception, and awareness
> Nowhere in them they find a place to rest on.
> Without a home they wander, dharmas never hold them,
> Nor do they grasp at them....
> [The Buddha] was not stationed in the realm which is free
>   from conditions,
> Nor in the things which are under conditions, but freely he
>   wandered without a home:
> Just so, without a support or a basis a bodhisattva is standing.

Awakening does not mean attaining some salvific wisdom—or, more precisely, the Tathagata's (Buddha's) wisdom is realizing that there is no such wisdom to be grasped. Instead, the mind does not fixate upon any particular forms, whether mental (e.g., ideologies, one's self-image, the Buddhadharma) or physical objects. Such identifications happen due to ignorance of the basic nondwelling nature of our awareness. Bodhisattvas live "without a support or a basis" because they do not cling, unlike the rest of us whose minds tend to grasp compulsively at one thing or another.

> The Dharma is not a secure refuge. He who enjoys
> a secure refuge is not interested in the Dharma
> but is interested in a secure refuge.
> —VIMALAKIRTI SUTRA

According to the eighteenth-century Japanese Zen master Hakuin, the difference between buddhas and other beings is like that between water and ice: just as there is no ice without water, so there are no sentient beings that are not buddhas—which suggests that deluded beings are simply "frozen" buddhas. The crucial point, then, is that awakening does not involve transcending this world, nor accepting it as it normally seems, but experiencing it in a nongrasping and therefore nondual way, which reveals that it is very different from the usual understanding.

> Let your mind come forth without fixing it anywhere.
> —Diamond Sutra

Perhaps the most important Chan (Zen) text of all—the Platform Sutra of the sixth patriarch Hui Neng—makes and remakes this same point about attachment and nonattachment: "When our mind works freely without any hindrance, and is at liberty to 'come' or to 'go,' we attain liberation." Such a mind "is everywhere present, yet it 'sticks' nowhere." Hui Neng emphasized that he had no system of Dharma to transmit: "What I do to my disciples is to liberate them from their own bondage with such devices as the case may need." Hui Hai, another Chan master who lived about a century later, elaborated on the nature of liberated mind:

> Should your mind wander away, do not follow it, whereupon your wandering mind will stop wandering of its own accord. Should your mind desire to linger somewhere, do not follow it and do not dwell there, whereupon your mind's questing for a dwelling place will cease of its own accord. Thereby, you will come to possess a nondwelling mind—a mind that remains in the state of nondwelling.... This full awareness in yourself of a mind dwelling upon nothing is known as having a clear perception of your own mind, or, in other words, as having a clear perception of your own nature. A mind which

dwells upon nothing is the Buddha-mind, the mind of one
already delivered, Bodhi-Mind, Un-created Mind.

In case we conclude that a capitalized Mind is something other than
our usual one, Huang Po deflates all delusions about its transcendence:

> Q: From all you have just said, Mind is the Buddha; but it is
> not clear as to what sort of mind is meant by this "Mind
> which is the Buddha."
> Huang Po: How many minds have you got?
> Q: But is the Buddha the ordinary mind or the Enlightened
> mind?
> Huang Po: Where on earth do you keep your "ordinary mind"
> and your "Enlightened mind"?

A FAMILIAR IMPLICATION is the Chan/Zen insistence that enlightenment is nothing more than realizing the true nature of the ordinary
activities of one's everyday mind. When Hui Hai was asked about his
own practice, he replied: "When I'm hungry I eat; when tired I sleep."
   The Pali texts of early Buddhism do not emphasize "everyday mind"
in the same way, for they often contrast the consciousness of an ordinary
person (*puthujjana*) with the liberated mind of an awakened *arahant*.
Yet there is the same focus on not-clinging, a notable example being
in the "Book of the Six Sense Bases" in the Samyutta Nikaya. There
the Buddha repeatedly teaches "the Dhamma for abandoning all." He
emphasizes that practitioners should develop dispassion toward the six
senses and their objects (including the mind and mental phenomena)
and abandon them, for that is the only way to end one's suffering.

> Through dispassion [his mind] is liberated. When it is liber-
> ated there comes the knowledge: "It's liberated." He under-
> stands: "Destroyed is birth, the holy life has been lived, what
> had to be done has been done, there is no more for this state
> of being."

Listening to this discourse, "the minds of the thousand *bhikkhus* were liberated from the taints by nonclinging." The absence of grasping is what liberates.

> Truly, is anything missing now?
> Nirvana is right here, before our eyes.
> This very place is the Lotus Land, this very body, the Buddha.
> —HAKUIN

Letting Go

Nonattachment is, of course, what we are practicing when we meditate. That is why meditation is such an important part of the Buddhist path. Because the self is composed of mostly habitual ways of thinking, feeling, acting, reacting, and so forth, it means that when I "let go" of them while meditating, I am deconstructing my sense of self—or, more precisely, the self is deconstructing, because it is not really something that "I" can do.

There are different ways to meditate because there are different ways to "let go." In Zen practice, which is what I am most familiar with, the focus is usually on "forgetting yourself," as described by the twelfth-century Japanese Zen master Dogen Kigen in a well-known passage from his *Shobogenzo*:

> To study Buddhism is to study yourself. To study yourself is to forget yourself. To forget yourself is to be awakened by the ten thousand things. When awakened by the ten thousand things, your body and mind as well as the body and mind of others drop away.
>
> —GENJOKOAN

This accords with what can happen during an intensive meditation retreat—for example, while working on the koan "Joshu's *Mu*" during a Zen *sesshin*. Here it is unnecessary to go into details, except to say that practitioners are instructed to repeat "*Muuu…*" mentally during breath exhalations. My constructed sense of self is normally sustained by the ways that my usual ways of thinking and acting interact. Focusing on "*Muuu…*" and cutting off everything else with "*Muuu…*" undermines that process. Instead of reacting to desires and thoughts ("Wouldn't a cold beer taste good right now!"), one lets them go by continually returning to "*Muuu…*"

Notice what this process does *not* involve. The point is not to cultivate blankness of mind by trying to push thoughts away, which creates a division between that which is pushing away and the thoughts that are pushed away. Instead, the principle is to concentrate on one thing—in this case, repeating "*Muuu…*" ceaselessly—in order to become absorbed into it and literally *become one with* it.

> Enlightenment is the dropping away of the self
> in the act of uniting with something.
> —Koun Yamada

At the beginning of this practice, I attempt to concentrate on *Muuu…* but am distracted by other thoughts and mental processes. As I persevere I become more able to focus on *Muuu…* and not wander away from it. What is described as the stage of ripeness and purity, when "both inside and outside naturally fuse," as Yasutani Roshi put it, is when there is no longer the sense of an "I" that is repeating the sound; there is only *Muuu…* This stage is sometimes described by saying that now *Muuu…* is doing *Muuu…*: it is *Muuu…* that sits, *Muuu…* that walks, *Muuu…* that eats, *Muuu…* that lies down to sleep. As the Buddha might say, in the *Muuuing* there is only the *Muuuing*.

Sometimes there arises the sensation of hanging over a precipice, dangling by a single thread. "Except for occasional feelings of uneasiness and despair, it is like death itself," according to Hakuin. The solution is to throw oneself completely into *Mu*. As Po Shan put it:

Bravely let go on the edge of the cliff. Throw yourself into the abyss with decision and courage. You only revive after death.

At this point, a teacher can help by cutting the last thread: an unexpected action, such as a blow or shout or even a few quiet words, may startle the student into letting go. Hakuin described the process: "All of a sudden he finds his mind and body wiped out of existence, together with the koan. This is what is known as 'letting go your hold.'" Many of the classical Zen stories tell of how a practitioner was enlightened by some sudden action or perception. In one instance, a monk was enlightened by the sound of a pebble striking bamboo. What happens in such cases is that the shock of the unexpected sensation causes it to penetrate to the very core of one's being—in other words, it is experienced nondually.

> There is a line a famous Zen master wrote at the time he became enlightened which reads: "When I heard the temple bell ring, suddenly there was no bell and no I, just sound." In other words, he no longer was aware of a distinction between himself, the bell, the sound, and the universe. This is the state you have to reach.... Stated negatively, it is the realization that the universe is not external to you. Positively, it is experiencing the universe as yourself.
>
> —YASUTANI ROSHI

In Dogen's case, awakening happened during meditation when his teacher Rujing berated another practitioner: "Body and mind must drop away." Hearing that, Dogen's did, and thereafter he sometimes referred to his "dropped-away body and mind." In the *Shobogenzo* Dogen describes his own experience by quoting the Chinese master Yang-shan: "I came to realize clearly that mind is nothing other than mountains, rivers and the great wide earth, the sun, the moon and the stars."

If one's usual sense of being separate from mountains and rivers is a delusion, then one's nonduality with them is not something that needs to be attained, just realized. And if the internal self is a construct, so is the external world, for if there is no inside (my mind), the outside is no longer outside (of an inside). Instead, each and every phenomenon that occurs, including you and me, expresses an immeasurably vast network of interacting processes, one of the multifarious and impermanent ways in which all the causes and conditions of the cosmos come together. There is no other reality outside these processes, nor do we need anything else.

Nisargadatta Maharaj has summarized this process most elegantly: "When I look inside and see that I am nothing, that's wisdom. When I look outside and see that I am everything, that's love. Between these two my life turns." Wisdom and compassion: the two wings of the dharma.

To realize that *I am nothing* (or, better, *no-thing*) is to become free, because there is no longer an insecure self inside that can never feel secure enough. Realizing that *I am everything* gives rise to compassion for others who are not really separate from me. Wisdom lived is love. Usually we assume that spiritual liberation and a sense of responsibility for what is happening in the world are different, but Nisargadatta reveals that they are two sides of same coin.

Something Infinite Behind Everything

> There was a child went forth every day,
> And the first object he look'd upon, that object he became.
> —WALT WHITMAN

Nisargadatta, a Vedantin, shows us something else as well: that this understanding of the path and its goal is not exclusively Buddhist. A cursory study of Advaita Vedanta, Taoism, Sufism, the Kabbalah, and Christian mysticism reveals that Buddhism does not have a corner on the Dharma. Each of these paths has its own distinctive way of articulating what is to be done and describing what happens, yet Buddhism's own emphasis on a "higher truth" that can never be grasped conceptually reminds us not to disparage other fingers pointing at the moon. This is crucial in a globalizing world where different religions cannot avoid rubbing shoulders with each other, and where the biggest challenge and opportunity for each of them becomes the beliefs and practices of the others.

I emphasize this because other spiritual traditions can help us understand how the world is transfigured when experienced nondually. Although the succinct descriptions of Yang-shan and Nisargadatta are memorable, I know of none more informative or moving than that of the seventeenth-century English clergyman and poet Thomas Traherne in his *Centuries of Meditations*. The account I have in mind is a bit long, and the language somewhat archaic, but it deserves reproduction in full because his depiction is so precise and suggestive. However, two words in the first sentence need some explaining. An old meaning of "corn" is "grain," which is why Traherne can say that the corn he saw was wheat. And "orient" here means "iridescent" or "lustrous," one of several references to the luminosity of the world he describes so lovingly.

Here it is, one of the classic passages of world spirituality:

> The corn was orient and immortal wheat, which never should be reaped, nor was ever sown. I thought it had stood from everlasting to everlasting. The dust and stones of the street were as precious as gold; the gates were at first the end of the world. The green trees when I saw them first through one of the gates transported and ravished me, their sweetness and unusual beauty made my heart to leap, and almost mad with ecstasy, they were such strange and wonderful things. The Men! O what venerable and reverend creatures did the aged seem! Immortal Cherubims! And young men glittering and sparkling Angels, and maids strange seraphic pieces of life and beauty! Boys and girls tumbling in the street, and playing, were moving jewels. I knew not that they were born or should die. But all things abided eternally as they were in

their proper places. Eternity was manifest in the Light of the Day, and something infinite behind everything appeared; which talked with my expectation and moved my desire. The city seemed to stand in Eden, or to be built in Heaven. The streets were mine, the temple was mine, the people were mine, their clothes and gold and silver were mine, as much as their sparkling eyes, fair skins and ruddy faces. The skies were mine, and so were the sun and moon and stars, and all the World was mine; and I the only spectator and enjoyer of it…. So that with much ado I was corrupted, and made to learn the dirty devices of this world. Which now I unlearn, and become, as it were, a little child again that I may enter into the Kingdom of God.

Traherne is quite wordy by Buddhist standards, and of course his words are not ones that Buddhists are likely to use. Yet his breathless account reverberates with Buddhist themes:

LIGHT AND ECSTASY: The world that Traherne describes is incredibly beautiful and blissful. The trees "transported and ravished" him; their unusual beauty made his heart leap "almost mad with ecstasy." And he points to what is special about that loveliness, referring again and again to the luminosity of things: the corn is "orient," the young men "glittering," angels "sparkling," and playing children are "moving jewels."

Nondualists in many traditions have emphasized the world's radiance: things that we usually perceive as solid objects now glow. A distinction that we normally take for granted—between physical objects and the light that they reflect—apparently no longer applies. The difference between them is actually one of the things that has been constructed; it is a product of our ways of thinking about the world, including the names that we assign to things. I overlook the radiance of a thing when I see it as simply "a cup." Usually I don't pay much attention to the cup: it's just something I use to drink my coffee. That is one of the ways I have learned to grasp the world, yet that habitual way of objectifying can also be unlearned. When we see things as they are, the visible world is no longer a collection of fixed, material, self-existing things but appears as a confluence of interacting, luminous *processes*. The cup on the table next to my computer is not a molded chunk of baked clay that just happens to be there. Its being-there is a glowing activity. And such processes are manifesting something, which Traherne later points to.

TIME: Religions tend to be preoccupied with an afterlife—with helping us qualify for an eternity in heaven with God, for example. Traherne describes a different type of "everlasting," which is not about surviving death and becoming immortal but experiencing here-and-now in a different way: dwelling in what is sometimes called *an eternal present*. His most wondrous line begins: "Eternity was manifest in the Light of the Day." The "immortal" wheat he sees was never sown and will never be reaped, having stood there "from everlasting to everlasting." In that regard Traherne doesn't distinguish between wheat, stones, trees, or humans: not only are they all radiant, each abides eternally insofar as it manifests the Light of the Day. In another *Centuries of Meditations* passage, just before this one, he declares: "All time was Eternity, and a perpetual Sabbath."

Many Buddhist teachings emphasize realizing the "deathless," and often "the unborn" as well. What would it mean, to transcend life and death? Do such claims refer to an afterlife? Traherne's account suggests a different perspective. It's the nature of all living creatures that they are born at a certain time and die at another time. Buddhism does not offer an escape from such impermanence. But if living beings, like all other things, are not self-existing—if they are interdependent processes that *manifest* something—then perhaps they cannot die insofar as they were never really born in the first place.

Manifest what? According to the Buddhist tantric tradition, our minds have three inalienable and inseparable aspects: they are luminous, blissful, and "empty" (*shunya*).

EMPTINESS: "Eternity was manifest in the Light of the Day, *and something infinite behind everything appeared*." Traherne's account does not mention God, except at the very end when he refers to becoming a little child again so that he might enter the Kingdom of God. The only other place in this passage where he perhaps alludes to God, or to some other spiritual reality, is this "something infinite." We are reminded of a better-known aphorism by William Blake: "If the doors of perception were cleans'd, everything would appear as it really is, infinite. For man has closed himself up, till he sees all things thro' narrow chinks of his cavern."

What is striking about this infinity for both Traherne and Blake is that it does not seem to be something that exists separately from the things they perceive. They see things *as* infinite. To rephrase the Heart Sutra: although forms are "empty" in the sense that things do not self-exist but are *manifesting* infinity, it's also true that the infinity they manifest is not something that is ever experienced in itself, apart from the forms it assumes.

> Importance is derived from the immanence
> of infinitude in the finite.
> —ALFRED NORTH WHITEHEAD

Mahayana Buddhist teachings sometimes talk about "the nonduality of emptiness (*shunyata*) and appearance." There is an important difference between how things usually appear to us, and what they really are. But the term "appearance" can be misleading insofar as it seems to imply that the world we normally perceive is nothing more than a dream-like illusion. Traleg Kyabgon Rinpoche explains this well:

> "Appearance" is a funny sort of word. It means some kind of surface thing, but with something else called "reality" that is behind it. "Presence" is a much better word. Something is presenting by itself, whose essence is emptiness. What appears is the phenomenal world, but it is empty because it has no real substance.

Presence is perhaps the best English word to describe what Traherne is pointing at. What we normally perceive as solid objects is the luminous *presencing* of something not-finite, unbounded. This infinite has no name or form of its own: in itself it is literally nothing, or, better, a no-thing that therefore can presence in many different ways. William Blake wrote that "eternity is in love with the productions of time"; in Buddhist terms, the "empty" infinite is in love with the ways it presences.

And among the ways that empty infinity presences are you and me. Realizing that "I" manifest a no-thing greater than myself—that that infinity is also behind me, or *within me*—is an essential insight.

TRANSCENDENCE: I mentioned earlier that religions often postulate a cosmological dualism: the duality between this created world and God in heaven is one common example, and the Buddhist distinction between samsara (this world of suffering) and nirvana (the Buddhist goal) is another. Traherne, however, does not allude to any other reality that transcends the magnificent world he describes, which is nothing other than the true nature of our world. The implication is that *this* is ultimate reality. If it transcends the way we usually experience this world, it is still *this world*. In Buddhist terms, the place we normally experience as a realm of suffering is not other than what we seek— nirvana itself, the Pure Land—when we see this place, right here, as it really is. Traherne makes this point by referring to Eden and Heaven: the town he tells us about, which usually appears so commonplace and unremarkable, now "seemed to stand in Eden, or to be built in Heaven." There's no need to aspire to anyplace else, for one doesn't need anything more.

> There are no unsacred places;
> there are only sacred places
> and desecrated places.
> —WENDELL BERRY

NONDUALITY: Traherne's account builds upon itself until it reaches a climax: "The streets were mine, the temple was mine, the people were mine, their clothes and gold and silver were mine, as much as their sparkling eyes, fair skins and ruddy faces. The skies were mine, and so were the sun and moon and stars, and all the World was mine; and I the only spectator and enjoyer of it." What are we to make of this mineness? Was his experience solipsistic?

Solipsism is the belief that the only reality is the self, yet that claim can be understood in different ways, depending on how one understands what the self really is. Buddhism emphasizes that there is no self, but if the basic problem is a sense of separate self confronting that which is other than itself—inside vs. outside—there may be no difference at all between an experience of all-self and the experience of no-self. What is important in both cases is that one transcends the usual dualism between an alienated and anxious sense of self that is separate from but trapped within an external, objectified world.

> You never know the world aright till the Sea floweth in your veins, till you are Clothed with the Heavens, and Crowned with the Stars; And perceive yourself to be the Sole Heir of the Whole World; And more so then, because Men are in it who are every one Sole Heirs, as well as you. Till you are intimately Acquainted with that Shady Nothing out of which this World was made; Till your spirit filleth the whole World and the Stars are your Jewels; Till you love Men so as to Desire their Happiness with a thirst equal to the zeal of your own.
> —TRAHERNE, CENTURIES OF MEDITATION

THE FALL: Traherne's exalted depiction concludes with a sudden deflation. The experience he describes has been lost, for he "was corrupted, and made to learn the dirty devices of this world." Yet there is hope: those devices he can "unlearn, and become, as it were, a little child again that I may enter into the Kingdom of God." The allusion is to Matthew 18:3, where Jesus says: "Truly I tell you, unless you change and become like little children, you will never enter the kingdom of heaven." This verse is often understood to refer to where we might go after we die, but we do well to remember something else Jesus reputedly said: "behold, the kingdom of God is in your midst." (This version is in Luke 17:21; more familiar to most of us is the King James version: "the kingdom of God is within you.") In the context of everything else that Traherne has just written, his desire to enter the Kingdom of God should surely be understood in the same way. The point is not to attain some otherworldly salvation but to "return" to the beautiful, luminous, blissful, eternal, nondual heavenly world he so poetically depicts.

"Return" is in scare-quotes because he has not really lost it. That is because his experience was a glimpse into what it really is, whether or not we are perceiving it that way. Having had a taste of it, Traherne knows what he has to do: to unlearn the "dirty devices of this world"— the world, that is, as normally experienced by "corrupted" people. What does he mean by corruption and the world's dirty devices? We may suppose that he is referring to immoral behavior, and that dirty devices are the ways people deceive and abuse each other. Yet corruption here might also include the types of delusion that the nondualist traditions emphasize. Delusions collude with cravings to reify the sense of a self that feels separate from the world it is "in." Grasping at things in the world, we lose our birthright: the world that Traherne so tenderly portrays. But we can always return to it, because it is always there. It becomes here whenever we open up to it.

NOTICE, HOWEVER, what Traherne does not mention. He tells us what he saw, but did he also hear differently? (T. S. Eliot: "Music heard so deeply that there is no music, but you are the music, while it lasts.") What about his bodily awareness? His experience of thinking? Traherne himself was one of those presences with something infinite behind it (in his case, within him), but he does not share those dimensions of this experience. Nor should we assume that his account exhausts the possibilities that may open up as we become more aware of our own empty infinity.

Implications

This way of understanding the spiritual path and its fruits raises some important issues, which will be addressed in the rest of this book.

First, is such a nondualist perspective compatible with what modern science has discovered? Needless to say, it seems quite inconsistent with the materialist and reductionist paradigm that has been so successful in explaining the world and bending it to our will—a worldview, however, that an increasing number of contemporary physicists and biologists no longer find persuasive. Many scientists, like most of us, still live in a Newtonian world, but Einstein's relativity theories and the paradoxes of quantum mechanics have revealed that the world is a much stranger place.

And nothing about it is stranger than the integral role of consciousness. We usually assume that we are "in" the objective world in much the same way as other physical objects are, yet the experimental evidence is unambiguous: what we experience as reality does not become "real" until it is perceived. Consciousness is the agency that collapses the quantum wave into an object, which until then exists only in potential. According to Erwin Schrödinger, the father of quantum theory (and an early exponent of Buddhism and Vedanta), in his book *Mind and Matter*: "The world is given to me only once, not one existing and one perceived. Subject and object are only one. The barrier between them cannot be said to have broken down as a result of recent experience in the physical sciences, for this barrier does not exist.... The material world has only been constructed at the price of taking the self, that is, mind, out of it, removing it; mind is not part of it."

> A physicist is the atom's way of knowing about atoms.
> —George Wald

The revolution in physics has spilled over into biology. In particular, reductionist understandings of the evolutionary process have become questionable. Evolutionary biologists such as Elisabet Sahtouris and

Bruce Lipton, along with cosmologists such as Brian Swimme and the "geologian" Thomas Berry, and now many others, have been developing a "new story" that offers an account of our origins that not only is scientifically sound but has important implications for how we understand Buddhism. This innovative account of cosmological and evolutionary development provides a fresh perspective on some basic Buddhist teachings, while, from the other side, a Buddhist perspective clarifies some aspects of the new story and adds to it. Their dialogue is the topic of the next part of this book.

Another issue raised by this way of understanding Buddhism is its social and ecological implications. The biggest lack in Traherne's account is perhaps something that he would not consider a shortcoming—and that some contemporary teachers also do not emphasize. In Buddhist terms, the "higher truth" that he describes so well is sundered from the conventional "lower truth" that we are more familiar with. Traherne's heavenly world has no problems; each luminous thing is a way that "empty infinity" presences, including the children playing in the street... but do they go to bed hungry at night? Although everything manifests eternity in the Light of the Day, in his day many of those particular manifestations died before their second birthday. Yes, the "higher truth" is that they didn't really die because they had never been born; from the perspective of the lower truth, however, there is birth, and death, and suffering. Patriarchy and slavery were the norm in Traherne's time. His society was organized hierarchically, for the benefit of those at the top of the class pyramid— something that also seems to be increasingly true of our society.

If awakening involves transcending this suffering world, we can ignore its problems. If the Buddhist path is psychological therapy, we can focus on our own individual neuroses. Yet both of those approaches assume and reinforce the illusion that I am essentially separate from others, and therefore can be indifferent to what they are experiencing. If "I" am not separate from others, neither is my well-being separate from theirs. Today this means that we are called upon not only to help other individuals deconstruct their sense of separation (the traditional role of a bodhisattva) but also to help our society to reconstruct itself, to become more just and sustainable—and awakened. The relationship between personal transformation and social transformation is explored in the third part.

STORY

The story of cosmic evolution reveals to us the common origin, nature, and destiny shared by all human beings. It documents our essential kinship as no other story can do…. This story shows us in the deepest possible sense that we are all sisters and brothers—fashioned from the same stellar dust, energized by the same star, nourished by the same planet, endowed with the same genetic code, and threatened by the same evils. This story, more than any other, humbles us before the magnitude and complexity of creation. Like no other story it bewilders us with the improbability of our existence, astonishes us with the interdependence of all things, and makes us feel grateful for the lives we have. And not least at all, it inspires us to express our gratitude to the past by accepting a solemn and collective responsibility for the future.

—LOYAL RUE, *Everybody's Story*

If you think of ourselves as coming out of the earth, rather than having been thrown in here from somewhere else, you see that we are the earth, we are the consciousness of the earth. These are the eyes of the earth. And this is the voice of the earth.

—JOSEPH CAMPBELL, *The Power of Myth*

IT HAS BECOME obvious, to anyone who's paying attention, that we live in critical times. The most obvious challenges are ecological and economic but there are plenty of other problems that can be added to the mix, especially overpopulation. Our finite biosphere cannot indefinitely support an economic system that requires indefinite growth to avoid collapse, or a species whose exploding numbers seem to require such growth.

What is less obvious is that there is an even more fundamental problem underlying such crises: at their root is a defective *story* about who we are, what the world is, and our role within it. Perhaps the biggest problem with this story is that we don't usually realize it is a story; we see the world and ourselves through it, according to it, with the assumption that what we are experiencing is reality itself, rather than an account of it. It is very unlikely that we'll be able to address the other crises successfully unless we also realize what is dysfunctional about the worldview that predominates today—and challenge it with a better one.

Many people have been contributing to a new paradigm, and its basic features are becoming clear. (For starters, I recommend *The Universe Story* by Brian Swimme and Thomas Berry.) Yet to be noticed, however, is how compatible this evolving worldview is with the most important teachings of Buddhism. In fact, a Buddhist perspective can help to illuminate some of its most distinctive aspects. This depends, of course, on how we understand Buddhism, for this story also challenges Buddhism to distinguish its essential viewpoint from Iron Age mythologies that need to be reconsidered today.

> The old gods are dead or dying, and people everywhere
> are searching, asking: what is the new mythology to be,
> the mythology of this unified earth as of one harmonious being?
> —JOSEPH CAMPBELL

A Devalued World

Our modern world with its distinctive social and economic institutions emerged out of the fragmentation of Christianity in the sixteenth century, along with a scientific worldview that (as Laplace reputedly said) did not require the hypothesis of a deity to explain the universe. As God disappeared, or ascended into the clouds, we found ourselves in a *secular* world—that is, a reality no longer defined in terms of its relationship with some "higher" sacred realm. Everyday life in medieval times had been saturated with religion: churches and monasteries, daily prayers, mass and other sacraments, canon law, processions, public penances and pilgrimages, and of course the yearly calendar of holy days (the origin of our "holiday"). As the modern world developed, God continued to be important for most people, but increasingly he was understood to dwell in the heavens above and within the human heart, instead of playing a dominant role in everyday public life.

We cherish our freedom from the imposed authority of religious institutions, yet it has come at a price. God was the traditional source of goodness, value, and meaning: he not only created this earth, he told us why we were here and taught us how we should live while we are here. God provided a solution to our greatest fear, death, by situating our mortality within a larger spiritual context. Human suffering and striving were not accidental or irrelevant, for they served a vital role within the grand structure of the cosmos and affected our ultimate destiny.

Charles Darwin's great contribution was not the discovery of evolution—that species evolved was widely accepted by the time he published the *Origin of Species*—but a naturalistic explanation for how that occurred. He thereby refuted the last remaining "proof" for God's existence: the "argument from design." The revolution that Darwin initiated meant that a supremely intelligent and all-powerful Being was no longer necessary to create the extraordinarily complex organisms, including us, that compose the web of life. Evolution by natural selection doesn't need a God to direct it.

That final stroke stranded us, for better and worse, in a desacralized world that has lost the source of its meaning, without a binding moral code to regulate how we relate to each other. The new secular universe, ruled by impersonal physical laws, seems indifferent to us and our fate. Human beings serve no function in the grand scheme of things, which means that we have no role to play except perhaps to enjoy ourselves as much as we can, while we can, if we can.

> Man at last knows that he is alone in the unfeeling immensity
> of the universe, out of which he has emerged only by chance.
> —JACQUES MONOD

Social Darwinism

Although the goodness, meaning, and value guaranteed by God have disappeared for many of us, our need for them has not, because we can't live without some version of them. If they are not provided by a God (or something equivalent that transcends this created world) we must find them here, by figuring it out for ourselves. What can fill the vacuum?

Inevitably, many people, scientists and nonscientists alike, have attempted to derive answers from science itself. Darwinism, in particular, opened the door for many new speculations about our human nature.

Soon after the *Origin of Species* was published, Darwin's theory was appropriated to justify the evolution of a new type of industrial economy. It was not Darwin himself but his Victorian contemporary Herbert Spencer who coined the term "survival of the fittest" and applied it to human society. Civilization came to be seen as another jungle environment where you must crawl over the next guy on your way to the top, or he will crawl over you. The value and meaning of life were largely understood in terms of survival and (primarily financial rather than reproductive) success. The basic unit of society is the individual, and morality is grounded in nothing more than social conditioning. Life is about what you can get and what you can get away with until you die. You're either a winner or a loser, and you don't want to be a loser. If you aren't successful, don't blame anyone else!

> With its rapid expansion, its exploitative methods, its desperate competition, and its preemptory rejection of failure, postbellum America was like a vast human caricature of the Darwinian struggle for existence and survival of the fittest. Successful business entrepreneurs apparently accepted almost by instinct the Darwinian terminology which seemed to portray the conditions of their existence.
> —RICHARD HOFSTADTER, *Social Darwinism in American Thought*

Referring to Herbert Spencer, Oliver Wendell Holmes doubted that "any writer of English except Darwin has done so much to affect our whole way of thinking about the universe." Industrial tycoons such as Andrew Carnegie and John D. Rockefeller embraced his philosophy. Carnegie's autobiography described how troubled and perplexed he had been about the collapse of Christian theology, until he read Darwin and Spencer. "I remember that light came as a flood and all was clear. Not only had I got rid of theology and the supernatural, but I had found the truth of evolution." He declared that Spencer's philosophy influenced him more than anything else, perhaps because it freed him from moral reservations about the pursuit of wealth that he had inherited from his more egalitarian Scottish relatives. (Spencer, however, did not approve of Carnegie's philanthropy, which interfered with the pitiless operation of social Darwinist principles.)

Rockefeller claimed that the fortune he ruthlessly accumulated through his giant Standard Oil Trust was "merely a survival of the fittest." In a Sunday-school address he justified his business principles by comparing them with cultivating a rose, which "can be produced in the splendor and fragrance which bring cheer to its beholder only by sacrificing the early buds which grow up around it. This is not an evil tendency in business. It is merely the working-out of a law of nature and a law of God." It is not clear whether the pruned rosebuds refer to

Rockefeller's competitors or his employees, but we can guess who the splendid, fragrant rose is.

> The real problem of humanity is that we have Paleolithic
> emotions, medieval institutions, and god-like technology.
> —E. O. WILSON

Basic to this ideology is the implication that I should pursue my own personal benefit even at the cost of your (or everyone else's) well-being. Understandably, then, social Darwinism is not a popular world-view today—though that might have something to do with the fact that social Darwinists may be more successful if they do not admit to what motivates them. Yet some recent adaptations have become more acceptable, such as Ayn Rand's influential "objectivism," whose "enticing prescription" Gore Vidal summarized as: "altruism is the root of all evil, self-interest is the only good." Ronald Reagan declared himself an admirer of her work, and Rand's philosophy has been increasingly popular among many libertarians and conservatives such as former Congressman Ron Paul, his son Senator Rand Paul, 2012 Vice Presidential candidate Paul Ryan (who credits her for inspiring him to get involved in public service), Supreme Court Justice Clarence Thomas, former South Carolina governor (now Senator) Mark Sanford, and former Federal Reserve chairman Alan Greenspan (a student and personal friend of Rand who said that he reads her novel *Atlas Shrugged* every year).

> Capitalism and altruism are incompatible....
> The choice is clear-cut: either a new morality of rational
> self-interest, with its consequences of freedom, justice,
> progress and man's happiness on earth—or the primordial
> morality of altruism, with its consequences of slavery,
> brute force, stagnant terror, and sacrificial furnaces.
> —AYN RAND

From a Buddhist perspective, social Darwinism in any of its incar-
nations rationalizes some very unsavory motivations, including the
"three poisons" of greed, aggression, and delusion—not least the delusion that I am separate from others, which is why I can pursue my own
interests with indifference to theirs. Many sociologists have pointed
out that a social application of Darwinism confuses impersonal biological processes with more reformable social arrangements, but whether
or not social Darwinism is objectively valid makes little difference,
in one way. If enough people believe in it and act according to it, it
becomes a self-fulfilling prophecy: we co-construct the world according to those principles and society does transform into something like
a Darwinist jungle. A crucial question, of course, is how much that has
happened today, and how much such a self-centered individualistic
worldview has contributed to our unsustainable ecological and economic situation.

The traditional rationale for capitalism has been Adam Smith's
understanding of a benevolent "invisible hand" that directs the marketplace: if all of us pursue what is best for us individually, that actually
works for the benefit of the whole. Since market exchange is a very efficient way to allocate resources, there is some truth to this. Nevertheless, when unconstrained by ethical norms or government regulation,
market relations readily end up becoming an economic perversion of
something Jesus taught: "To those that have, it shall be given—from
those that do not have, it shall be taken away." Economic forces need
to be contained within a moral or political structure that mitigates the
exploitative opportunities that inevitably arise.

Although Smith's invisible hand has become an established ideology,
used to argue for liberating free enterprise from the oppressive control
of government, I cannot help suspecting that maximizing the public
good is not the principle that actually motivates Wall Street, Big Oil, or
the politicians they own. Behind such rationalizations lurks an attitude
that does not usually want to draw attention to itself yet is generally
taken for granted in such circles: use your position to get whatever
you can. This motivation is hardly a new factor in human history, but

what *is* new and troubling is a widely promoted and socially acceptable worldview that celebrates it. Since we all want to feel good about what we do, greed too seeks a philosophy to justify itself, and social Darwinism, in one version or another, has been the convenient solution.

A notorious recent example of a social Darwinist is the former CEO of Enron, Jeffrey Skilling, who is now serving a long prison term for conspiracy, securities fraud, and insider trading. He declared that his favorite book was Richard Dawkins's *The Selfish Gene* and said that he understood neo-Darwinism to mean that ultimately selfishness was good because it weeded out losers and compelled survivors to become strong. (Dawkins said that Skilling misunderstood his book.)

> "Greed, for lack of a better word, is good. Greed is right.
> Greed works. Greed clarifies, cuts through, and
> captures the essence of the evolutionary spirit."
> —GORDON GECKO, IN *Wall Street*

Of course, misappropriating a Darwinian understanding of evolution has not been the only response to the disappearance of God-given meaning and value. Social Darwinism and its more contemporary versions accord nicely with the hedonism encouraged by an economic system that conditions us to find the meaning of our lives in neverending consumption. From a Buddhist perspective, however, consumerism promises a this-worldly salvation that it never quite provides: attractive advertisements are carefully crafted to keep us persuaded that the *next* thing we buy will make us happy.

Social Darwinism and consumerism can be understood as responses to the same deep-rooted problem: according to the prevalent scientific stories about cosmology and evolution, human beings, like other species, are a result of random DNA mutations. Virtually every premodern culture believed that their society had an important role to play in keeping the cosmos working, but now we know—or at least science seems to be telling us—that we have no such function; our existence is an accident and meaningless in the larger scheme of things. Perhaps it's no wonder, then, that we don't mind returning the compliment by trashing a world that seems so indifferent to us.

Whatever else Buddhism involves, it offers an alternative to consumerism and social Darwinism. What does it have to say about evolution?

> Human beings must have an epic, a sublime account
> of how the world was created and how humanity
> came to be part of it.... [Religious epics] confirm that
> we are part of something greater than ourselves.
> —LOYAL RUE, *Everybody's Story*

Creation Stories

The "geologian" Thomas Berry said that we are between stories—an uncomfortable place, to be sure, but nonetheless a good place to be if the old story has become dysfunctional.

According to the distinguished biologist E. O. Wilson, the new story we seek can be provided by evolution: "The true evolutionary epic, retold as poetry, is as intrinsically ennobling as any religious epic." But not if evolution is understood as merely the fortuitous result of random genetic mutations that occasionally make an organism more reproductively successful. Many biologists are now questioning this reductionist account, in ways that offer fresh possibilities for our inevitable questions about values and meaning. Any epic that can satisfy us must be consistent with what science is discovering about the origins and development of the universe, yet for an epic to be spiritual those discoveries must also help us understand how we fit in. Why we are here? What is our role? And this is precisely where a Buddhist perspective may have something special to offer.

> Evolution, then, is the creation myth of our age.
> —MARY MIDGELEY

> Buddhism is an evolutionary sport.
>
> —ROBERT THURMAN

Most religions have problems with evolution because scientific accounts seem to contradict their creation stories. The Buddha too offered a creation myth, sort of, in the Agganna Sutta, although it's not clear how literally it should be taken.

The sutta recounts a conversation between the Buddha and two young Brahmins who had been reviled for following the Buddha (who was of the warrior caste); their peers felt they should remember that Brahmins are superior to the other castes, for they are born from the mouth of the great god Brahma. The Buddha has an easy time with that claim, pointing out that Brahmins are conceived and born just like everyone else. What makes people superior is not the caste they are born into but how they live.

Then the Buddha presents a charming story about the origins of this world—not, strictly speaking, a creation myth that explains how the cosmos initially began, but an account of what happens when it periodically contracts and expands. When fully contracted, self-luminous mind-made beings glide through the air and feed on delight, but as the cosmos expands they become increasingly greedy and therefore gain bodies that become increasingly coarse. They also become competitive and ill-tempered, which means they need a ruler to control themselves.

The most important part of the story is what happens after this cosmic expansion, where the Buddha explains that the four castes differentiate because they decide to live in different ways. Instead of offering another mythological account, he provides a sociological one: in more contemporary terms, a simple but unmistakable example of what might be called social constructivism.

It is difficult to determine what the Buddha meant with the earlier, more fanciful part of this curious tale. It's also not clear whether Buddhism even needs a creation story. Elsewhere the Buddha emphasized that he was interested only in how suffering could be ended, not how it began. Perhaps Buddhism as a path of liberation does not require an explanation of how the world originated?

> My main interest is promoting ethics without touching religion. Ethics are universal values. We must find a way to promote the basic human values in a secular way without touching religion.
>
> —THE DALAI LAMA

This raises the issue of a *secular ethics*. For some years the Dalai Lama has been promoting a rational and humane approach to morality that does not rely on religious belief but instead focuses on universally shared values such as compassion. In a globalizing world riven by religious hostilities, this is a laudable and probably necessary project. Nevertheless, the cautionary example of social Darwinism shows how difficult it is to separate ethics from one's basic worldview, traditionally provided by religion. We normally derive how we should live, and how we want to live, from our views about what the world really is, including how it got to be the way it is and how we got to be the way we are. The bridge between ethics and worldview is one's understanding of our role within the world, which is an essential part of any story that can satisfy us.

As self-aware beings living in a mysterious universe, we need some explanation of our origins, whether mythological or scientific. The Judeo-Christian West was generally satisfied with a Biblical account until the scientific revolution, and if Buddhism has nothing specific to offer in this regard then most of us will continue to accept what modern science says about the matter—or what we think science is saying, since the paradoxes of relativity theory and quantum mechanics reveal that reality is more mysterious than the Newtonian world most of us take for granted. The Buddhist worldview as presented in the Agganna Sutta more or less assumes the commonly believed cosmology of that period, about 400 BCE, which describes vast cycles of evolution and devolution, expansion and contraction—curiously, more compatible with modern cosmology than anything in the Bible. One of the big challenges for contemporary Buddhism is to determine in what ways its fundamental worldview is compatible with recent scientific discoveries regarding cosmology and evolution, and how much it can contribute to our understanding of that developing story.

> Our knowing the epic of evolution
> bears on the evolution of the epic.
> —LOYAL RUE, *Everybody's Story*

A New Evolutionary Myth

For religions to remain relevant today, they must stop denying or minimizing or ignoring evolution. Instead of seeing it as conflicting with their own doctrines, they need to incorporate its story into the core of their own stories, considering not only the meaning of their own teachings in the light of evolution, but also the meaning of evolution in the light of their own teachings.

As David Sloan Wilson has pointed out, the most extraordinary fact about public awareness of evolution is not that half the people in the U.S. don't believe in it (surveys regularly report that more people believe in the virgin birth of Jesus) but that almost none of us have connected it to anything of importance in our lives. We need a new version (and vision) of the evolution story that relates scientific findings to the meaning of our personal lives and to the collective meaning of human life.

> All our sciences are the material that has to be mythologized.
> A mythology gives spiritual import—what one might call
> rather the psychological, inward import, of the world
> of nature round about us, as understood today.
> —JOSEPH CAMPBELL

Buddhism has no problem with evolution, which is consistent with its own emphasis on impermanence and insubstantiality. Nothing has any *svabhava* (literally "self-being") because everything is directly dependent on many other things, and thus indirectly on everything else. As Thich Nhat Hanh has expressed it, flowers are made up of nonflower elements: soil, water, sun, and so forth. This accords well with the biological understanding of how species evolve; one could say that each species is made up of its relations with other species and of other environmental interactions that it depends upon to survive and thrive. And if change is the only constant, the focus shifts from *being* to *becoming*, with profound implications.

One of the ways that language commonly misleads us is with the distinction between nouns and verbs, as in the subject and predicate of a proper sentence. The problem is not merely linguistic: in learning to speak grammatically we also learn to *see* that the world is composed of individual *things* that *act* (or don't act) in certain ways. Sometimes the distinction becomes absurd: what does the "it" refer to when we say, "It's raining"? From a Buddhist perspective, however, the world is not a collection of biological species and inanimate objects. It's a confluence of processes, and each of those processes is directly or indirectly dependent upon the many organic and inorganic processes that compose the biosphere.

> The universe is not a place where evolution happens,
> *it is* the evolution. It is not a stage on which dramas unfold,
> *it is* the unfolding drama itself.
> —LOYAL RUE, *Everybody's Story*

If the universe is not some*thing* that is evolving but *is* the evolutionary process itself, then another word to describe that development, in all its cosmological, biological, and cultural aspects, is *creativity*. Are the cosmic formation of galaxies, the biological ramification of speciating life forms, and the cultural development of human societies different manifestations of the same generative principle? Not as different things that the universe is making, which assumes the old duality between nouns and verbs, but as various transformations of a resourceful process that ceaselessly creates new physical, organic, and cultural forms.

According to the cosmologist Brian Swimme, the greatest scientific discovery of all time is that if you leave hydrogen gas alone (for almost fourteen billion years) "it turns into rosebushes, giraffes, and humans." The full process was a little more complicated: it took a while (apparently about 380,000 years) for the energy produced by the Big Bang to cool sufficiently to transform into matter—initially mostly hydrogen (the simplest atom), with lesser amounts of helium and lithium. Yet all that should not distract us from Swimme's point, which suggests a follow-up question: is this greatest of scientific discoveries also an important spiritual discovery? The key issue is what that implies about hydrogen gas, or rather that which became hydrogen gas (mostly) and since then has become everything else as well.

> American Indian lore speaks of three miracles.
> The first miracle is that anything exists at all.
> The second miracle is that living things exist.
> The third miracle is that living things exist that *know* they exist.
> —DUANE ELGIN, *The Living Universe*

What we usually think of as evolution—the genetic variability that generates new and more complex life forms—is only the middle of three progressive developments. The first stage started with the Big Bang (or "the great Flaring Forth," according to Brian Swimme), although the nature of that abrupt beginning has recently become more controversial. Cosmological research over the last few decades supports the possibility that the Big Bang may not have been unique; theoretical physicists such as Andrei Linde and Alan Guth have hypothesized that our "multiverse" is a self-generating fractal that periodically sprouts other inflationary universes—that is, other Big Bangs. That possibility remains contentious, and fortunately largely irrelevant to our purposes, except that a self-generating fractal universe implies even greater dimensions of self-organizing creativity.

In order for the second stage of evolution to begin, the vast amounts of hydrogen created at the Big Bang needed to transform into heavier elements. Gravity collapsed clouds of gas into stars, and as their superdense cores ignited, hydrogen fused into the heavier atoms of the periodic table, including carbon, oxygen, nitrogen, sulfur, phosphorus, and calcium—the other elements most necessary for life as we know it. When these stars and supernovas later exploded, those elements were scattered to eventually recoalesce into secondary solar systems such as our own.

Along with hydrogen, the heavier elements provided the material basis for the emergence of self-replicating and self-evolving species on earth, beginning about four billion years ago, and the appearance of human beings approximately 200,000 years ago.

Last but not least has been the evolution of human societies—the cultural developments that have been necessary to produce "highly evolved" human beings such as Shakyamuni Buddha and more recent examples such as Gandhi and Einstein.

> Our bodies are made of stardust;
> our souls are made of stories.
> —Tom Rhodes

The later processes that comprise the third stage depend upon the earlier ones. Life, as we know it, requires elements such as carbon and oxygen, and of course human civilization is the development of a particular species that depends upon many other species. Although we usually distinguish biological from cultural evolution, in his book *Nonzero* Robert Wright points out that they progress in parallel ways: both involve growth in the depth and scope of complexity, including the ability to store and process data. The important point is that, "like individual organisms, societies convert energy into material structures."

Note that there is no creation "out of nothing" (except perhaps the mysterious Big Bang itself). Each new process depends upon possibilities created by previous ones. As Buddhism emphasizes, everything is interdependent, arising and passing away according to conditions.

> God sleeps in stone, breathes in plants,
> dreams in animals, and awakens in man.
> —Hindu proverb

So how shall we understand the progression of these three "nested" stages? We are most familiar with two stories that attempt to explain it. One of them involves belief in a Being outside these processes who is directing it. According to recent polls, well over eighty percent of Americans either don't accept evolution at all, or believe in "intelligent design"—that God is managing the process.

In contrast to guided evolution, most biologists see these developments as more haphazard: the evolution of species is due to random DNA mutations, some of which enable the organism to be more reproductively successful in its specific environment.

Is our choice between intelligent design and haphazard mutation, or is there a third alternative?

On the face of it, the term "random" is descriptive yet a value judgment is often implied. Scientists don't like randomness because they look for predictable patterns. Einstein was unhappy about the indeterminacy revealed by quantum mechanics, which describes the behavior of subatomic particles in terms of probabilities rather than cause and effect. He famously remarked that "God does not play dice with the universe," but perhaps he missed the point here. As a theoretical physicist, he sought to discover regularities that could be quantified into scientific laws, yet at the quantum level they do not seem to operate. Freeman Dyson, another respected physicist, offered an explanation: "Matter in quantum mechanics is not an inert substance but an active agent, constantly making choices between alternative possibilities.... It appears that mind, as manifested by the capacity to make choices, is to some extent inherent in every electron."

In other words, what we perceive as randomness implies some degree of freedom, and freedom involves consciousness, even at the subatomic level. What does that suggest about "random" DNA mutations?

Contrary to what conventional science and religion have been telling
us, evolution is neither random nor predetermined but rather
an intelligent dance between organism and environment.
—BRUCE H. LIPTON AND STEVE BHAERMAN, *Spontaneous Evolution*

Perhaps it is no coincidence that the two most common options—
God or chance mutations—reproduce what has been the dominant
duality of the Western tradition: mind vs. matter. Both explanations
take that dualism for granted but privilege opposite sides. Theists
believe that God created the universe (a version of consciousness
creating matter), while materialists believe that consciousness arises
only when organisms develop to a certain complexity (matter creates
consciousness).

Non-Western philosophical traditions offer different worldviews
that escape this bipolar dualism. For example, the Chinese concept
of *qi* (or *ch'i*: the principle that underlies acupuncture and martial
arts) and the Indian concept of *prana* (the principle behind much of
Indian medicine) both refer to a "life force" or "energy flow" that is
more than matter but less than mind. Similar conceptions are found
in many other cultures, including the Polynesian *mana*, Hebrew *ruah*,
and Tibetan *lung*. None of these assumes our common Western way
of sharply distinguishing between matter, energy, and consciousness,
which are classical concepts that can be traced back to Aristotle. What
might these less dualistic worldviews imply about the evolutionary
process?

The world has not been printed out from an initial code.
It is the world that has created a new world.
—PAUL R. FLEISHMAN

According to the eminent biologist Theodosius Dobzhansky, evolution is neither random nor predetermined but *creative*. Another
respected evolutionary biologist, Elisabet Sahtouris, describes evolution

as an intelligent, improvisational dance. The dance is not supervised by a dancing-master who programs the dancers' movements, but neither are the steps arbitrary. Rather, the dance evolves as the dancers discover new possibilities, in a ballet whose choreography never ceases to transform and (usually) complexify. In other words, the cosmos *self-organizes*.

> The central quality of the evolutionary process is creative emergence....
> Living systems, from the smallest microbes to the largest organisms,
> exhibit self-organization; all of life is basically defined
> by this self-generating, self-maintaining criterion.
> —STUART KAUFFMAN

What did Brian Swimme say about what happens to hydrogen gas if we leave it alone? There is no place in the familiar reductionist model—the predominant scientific paradigm—for self-organization. According to that understanding of evolution, biological transformations are the result of material processes operating according to impersonal and fixed physical laws. But what if, instead of reducing biology to physics and viewing the cosmos as a machine, we turn that around and understand the physical universe according to a biological model?

> If you want to change the world,
> you have to change the metaphor.
> —JOSEPH CAMPBELL

In fact, there is a fundamental problem with the mechanistic paradigm, as Elisabet Sahtouris has pointed out in *EarthDance*:

> Scientific distinctions between mechanics and organics have been blurred because we ignored the fact that mechanisms are, by definition, the purposive constructions of their inventors, and therefore cannot exist as natural entities evolving in purposeless (nonteleological) nature. Our whole scientific concept of nature as a mechanism was derived

from a Cartesian scheme that was logically complete because it included God as inventor. But to maintain that nature is mechanism after repudiating God and purpose constitutes a severe logical flaw at the heart of Western science.

Think of a machine, any machine... What makes it a machine? In analyzing an organism into its component parts, and then trying to explain its functioning as if it were a machine, we overlook the fact that our conception of a machine presupposes a machine-maker: an intelligence and intentionality distinct from the machine it designs and constructs. That made sense as long as God was understood to have created the universe according to his own plan and purposes. Without God, however, the mechanistic model of explanation breaks down. *Any machine that constantly reorganizes itself, creating more complex structures as evolving parts of itself, is not a machine.* It is better understood as an *organism*.

Does that mean that the universe is *alive*? According to the philosopher Ervin Laszlo, this newly emerging paradigm about self-organization also happens to be the traditional premodern paradigm:

> At the cutting edge of contemporary science a remarkable insight is surfacing: the universe, with all things in it, is a quasi-living, coherent whole. All things in it are connected.... A cosmos that is connected, coherent and whole recalls an ancient notion that was present in the tradition of every civilization: it is an enchanted cosmos.... We are part of each other and of nature. We are a conscious part of the world, a being through which the cosmos comes to know itself.... We are at home in the universe.

That we are "a being through which the cosmos comes to know itself" suggests that we are an integral part of it, that we have a role to play. Then the cosmos is something more than the place where we happen to reside; it makes more sense to say that we are an organ of the universe. But bodily organs have functions; then what is ours, in the larger scheme of things?

One of the main sources of our estrangement from nature—the supposedly scientific discovery that life is meaningless, because we, like other species, exist only due to the operation of indifferent physical laws and the accidents of genetics—becomes questionable.

> We are beyond reductionism: life, agency, meaning, value, and even consciousness and morality almost certainly arose naturally, and the evolution of the biosphere, economy, and human nature are stunningly creative often in ways that cannot be foretold.... In this partial lawlessness is not an abyss, but unparalleled freedom, unparalleled creativity.
> —STUART KAUFFMAN, *Reinventing the Sacred*

A growing body of biological research supports this less mechanical and more organismic understanding of the evolutionary process. Mainstream evolutionary theory can only understand genetic mutations as haphazard: a few of them turn out to be beneficial, but the process is hit or miss, without any purpose or intention involved. This is a claim that has been tested in experiments with bacteria, which are an ideal subject since they reproduce so quickly. Research biologists such as Lynn Margulis and Mae-Wan Ho have established that colonies of bacteria respond to changes in the environment much faster than could be explained by chance mutations. The bacteria seemed to exhibit intelligence and intentionality in the ways they were able to modify their own genetics in order to adapt to new circumstances.

A well-known experiment was conducted by the geneticist John Cairns in the late 1980s. He isolated a strain of the bacterium *E. coli* that was unable to digest lactose. When their only food source was lactose, however, the bacteria quickly mutated and became able to metabolize it, due to what Cairns termed "purposive mutation" and others have called "adaptive mutation." Another researcher, Barry Hall, found that something similar happened when *E. coli* were placed in a solution of salicin: the colony became able to metabolize the salicin because of two otherwise rare genetic mutations that happened at a rate thousands of times faster than predicted.

These experiments have been replicated many times. When the alternative is starvation and extinction, a will to survive apparently motivates a large surge in various genetic mutations, until some of those mutations provide what is sought. Significantly, no consistent pattern has been observed in the sequences of the successful mutations. In that respect the process is random, or (as I prefer) *groping*, but as soon as the needed mutation appears, the surge in mutations stops. Such research seems to support the conclusion that organisms are capable of responding to dynamic changes in their environment by proactively altering their own genetic code. In short, this evidence supports a more dynamic, self-organizing understanding of the evolutionary process.

> Life is more impressive and less predictable than any
> "thing" whose nature can be accounted for
> solely by "forces" acting deterministically.
> —LYNN MARGULIS AND DORION SAGAN, *What Is Life?*

The broader implication of this new paradigm is that we can view evolution as the creative groping of a self-organizing cosmos that is becoming more self-aware. Does it *want* to become more self-aware? In *The Universe Story* Berry and Swimme make the point more poetically: "The mind that searches for contact with the Milky Way is the very mind of the Milky Way galaxy in search of its inner depths." What does this imply about Walt Whitman, for example, admiring a beautiful sunset? Berry and Swimme: "Walt Whitman is a space the Milky Way fashioned to feel its own grandeur." Instead of our eyes being the product of a mechanistic process driven by random mutations, can they be understood as having been created by the cosmos, in order to be able to perceive itself?

The human can be defined as that being in whom the universe reflects
on and celebrates itself in a special mode of conscious awareness....
We are the self-consciousness of the universe.

—THOMAS BERRY

A New Buddhist Story

This is where things get very interesting, from a Buddhist perspective. A self-organizing cosmos would shed light on some age-old Buddhist questions. If enlightenment involves realizing that there is no self, who (or what) becomes enlightened? For that matter, if (as Buddhist teachings claim) there has never been a self, then who is it that *wants* to become enlightened? Can my subjective desire to awaken be understood in a more nondual way as the urge of the universe itself to become self-aware, in me and as me?

We cannot escape the fact that the world we know is
constructed in order (and thus in such a way as to be able)
to see itself.... But in order to do so, evidently it must first
cut itself up into at least one state which sees,
and at least one other state that is seen.

—G. SPENCER BROWN

We are reminded again of Dogen's description of his own awakening: "I came to realize clearly that mind is no other than mountains and rivers and the great wide earth, the sun and the moon and the stars." According to one Mahayana account, the Buddha was enlightened when he looked up from his meditations and saw the morning star (Venus), whereupon he declared: "I am awakened together with the whole of the great earth and all its beings." It's not that every living being became enlightened in the same way that he did at that moment, but that his own personal awakening was an achievement of the whole. Awakening, then, involves realizing that "I" am not inside my body, looking out through my eyes at a world that is separate from me. Rather, "I" am what the whole universe is doing, right here and now.

> The mind that sees and understands the star
> is no less radiant than its object.
> —PAUL R. FLEISCHMAN

This understanding of awakening is not some fanciful reinterpretation of the Buddhist tradition. It is consistent with many of the metaphors and conceptualizations that have traditionally been used to describe the experience; in fact, it illuminates them. As mentioned in part I, Dogen emphasized the importance of "forgetting" oneself, in order to "let go." It's not quite right to say that one "lets go" of oneself, for that way of expressing the process is still dualistic: *who* lets go of *what?* Instead, the (sense of) self *lets go* and "the bottom drops out of the bucket," according to a Zen metaphor. Where does one fall to? The answer was discussed in part I: one doesn't. There is no such ground— or, if you prefer, the only ground that remains is groundlessness itself. "I" become aware that I am manifesting something that I can never grasp. It's as if I am a spring of water bubbling up from I-know-not-where, or the surface of a sea with unfathomable depths. When I see (or hear, or think) something, who is *doing* the seeing, etc.? To awaken is to realize the sense in which I can never know, and why I do not need to know.

> Our practice is not to clear up the mystery.
> It is to make the mystery clear.
> —ROBERT AITKEN

There is a paradox here. The Advaita Vedantic tradition uses the term *Brahman* to claim that everything is One, but what would it be like for me to *experience* everything as One? That would be dualistic, because there would still be an experiencer who is aware *of* the One-ness. I can *describe* the world as One, but that conceptualization views the world from "outside the One," as it were. To actually experience the One would be to merge with it, in which case there would not even be a One; instead, there would be what Buddhism refers to, more phenomenologically, as *shunyata*.

> All evolution is the progressive self-revelation
> of the One to himself.
> —SRI AUROBINDO

A self-organizing cosmos has another important Buddhist implication. If the universe is not some thing that evolves, but is the evolutionary process itself, we cannot reductively say that it is basically composed of matter, or energy, or even the plasma created at the mysterious "great Flaring Forth." Rather, the universe is the totality of the ongoing creative process, irreducible to specific constituents that we might try to pick out. And this is quite compatible with some basic Buddhist teachings, which have a special term for this generativity.

That term, again, is *shunyata*, usually translated as "emptiness"— although not without some loss of meaning. According to the usual explanation, *shunyata* refers to the fact that everything is "empty" of self-nature: nothing has any existence of its own, for each phenomenon in the universe is dependent upon many other things, and is therefore a function of a network that is always changing, a temporary manifestation of the way that innumerable causal processes are interacting.

Yet that explanation by itself is incomplete. Shunyata can also be understood more dynamically as "unlimited potentiality," because their lack of fixed being is what enables such processes—including evolutionary processes—to transform into other processes. According to Shunryu Suzuki, *shunyata* "does not mean voidness. There is something, but that something is something which is always prepared for taking some particular form." A something that does not have any fixed form of its own and is therefore able to transmute into another particular form, according to the possibilities available in a situation.

We are like clouds who do not realize
that we are made of the sky.
—DUANE ELGIN, *The Living Universe*

We are now approaching the heart of the matter. Shunyata is not only a metaphor for the irreducible dynamic creativity of the cosmos, ceaselessly generating new forms out of itself; it also describes the true nature of my own and your own "nondwelling" mind, which is supple in its ability to adapt and assume any particular form because it lacks any fixed form of its own. Does awakening, then, involve realizing that one's own true nature is not different from that of the entire universe? That my own "groundless ground" is in fact the ground of the whole cosmos?

...those who turn about
and bear witness to self-nature,
self-nature that is no-nature,
go far beyond mere doctrine.
—HAKUIN

There is an intriguing verse in Nagarjuna's *Mulamadhyamakakarika* that seems to make that very point: "The self-existence of a Buddha is the self-existence of this very cosmos. The Buddha is without a self-existent nature; the cosmos too is without a self-existent nature." Although the apparent paradox is charming, the implication is clear; the "self-nature" of both awakened beings and the entire universe is that neither has any fixed, determinate self-nature. And since awakening does not involve gaining a new nature, just simply realizing what you have always been, this assertion can be expanded: your true nature—your no-self-nature, right here and now—is not different from the no-self nature of the cosmic process.

The incessant self-organizing creativity that produces all things can never be perceived or comprehended in itself, apart from its particular

manifestations. And yet in the most important sense we can know it—
we *do* know it—because we *are* it. The same generative process that
produces solar systems and countless plant and animal species is also
taking form as this sentence that I am writing, and as the thought that
forms in your mind as you read it. To realize that the activity of your
own mind is another expression of the cosmic creative process is to
find yourself truly at home in the universe.

> The universe shivers with wonder
> in the depths of the human.
> —BRIAN SWIMME

Progress

What does this imply about the new evolutionary story and our role
in the cosmic process? Can we congratulate ourselves that we are the
goal of that development? Or, more modestly, at least a product of evolutionary progress?

The basic problem with evaluating biological progressivism is that
the term is not merely descriptive; it is unavoidably evaluative. To
describe something as progressing is to assert that its later forms are
somehow better than the earlier ones. One of the most outspoken crit-
ics of this belief was Stephen Jay Gould, who argued that any perception of progress in evolution is a delusion based on human arrogance.

According to the Bible humans are unique. God said, "Let us make
man in our image, in our likeness, and let them rule over the fish of the
sea and the birds of the air, over the livestock, over all the earth, and
over all the creatures that move along the ground" (Genesis 1:26). That
creation story and the impact of social Darwinism show the danger
in anointing ourselves as the pinnacle of creation. But understanding
ourselves as superior to all other species, which therefore exist only for
our benefit, is not the only way to understand progress.

Empirically, an evolutionary tendency toward increasing complexity
and greater awareness is difficult to overlook. It is undeniable that a

number of significant biological traits have developed and improved over time, most noticeably the better information-processing abilities provided by larger brains. The evolutionary biologist Jeffrey Schloss cites a number of developing traits that include "homeostatic control, sensory acuity, behavioral and locomotive freedom, various measures of complexity at cellular, organismal, and social levels, body mass and lifespan, per capita parental investment, and capacity for intersubjective awareness and inter-organismal attachment." That evolution has a *direction* is suggested by the fact that multicellularity (the necessary foundation for all "higher" life forms) was developed separately by perhaps as many as ten different species; that the ability to fly was invented at least three different times; and that eyesight (the most difficult sense to develop, one would imagine) evolved independently dozens of times. One way or another—or is it one way *and* another?—such complexifications seem to have been inevitable, given favorable conditions.

Not all biologists are uncomfortable talking about evolution as progress. According to E. O. Wilson, progress "is a property of the evolution of life as a whole by almost any conceivable intuitive standard, including the acquisition of goals and intentions in the behavior of animals. It makes little sense to judge it irrelevant.… An undeniable trend of progressive evolution has been the growth of biodiversity by increasing command of earth's environment."

> The evidence of progress and directionality
> in biological evolution is clear enough
> if the living world is considered as a whole.
> —THEODOSIUS DOBZHANSKY

The challenge is to understand progression in a way that does not fall into the hubris that worried Gould, which has been used to justify ideologies such as racism—for instance, the Nazi glorification of Aryans as superior to Semites. Such hubris is not a peril that tempts us, however, but a habit we developed a long time ago: the way that we as a species relate to other species reveals our sense of supremacy, including our God-given right (or at least our technological power) to use and abuse them any way we like. On the other hand, we also want to acknowledge that there is something valuable about increased consciousness and the life forms that possess it—such as primates and especially human beings. To view *Homo sapiens sapiens* (admittedly, there's hubris in the name we've given ourselves) as distinctive is not just collective vanity but a recognition of something that seems significant even if we don't quite understand what it means.

Progress does not necessarily mean teleology: that there is an endpoint to the evolutionary process. An example of such a final goal is the "omega point" that Pierre Teilhard de Chardin argued for in *The Phenomenon of Man*. He believed that the universe is evolving toward a condition of maximum complexity and consciousness, and that attaining this state would in effect become the end of history.

Buddhism offers a different perspective on progress. Although bodhisattvas take a vow to help all living beings enter nirvana, that project need not be understood teleologically, in the sense that there will come a time when all beings have become fully awakened. Rather than focusing on some future endpoint, the bodhisattva vow indicates a *direction* to one's life, an undertaking that answers the ultimate question about the focus and meaning of life right here and now. One can work for the betterment of the world without believing that there will come a time when the suffering caused by greed, aggression, and delusion no longer occurs. In the same way, evolutionary development in complexity and awareness does not necessarily imply that that process will ever complete itself. In fact, it's hard to imagine what completion could mean.

Nevertheless, traditional Buddhist teachings do not seem to support the idea of progress any more than Stephen Jay Gould does. On the contrary, enlightenment is usually understood to involve realizing something impervious to time in the sense that it does not change: either an unconditioned dimension (according to a common understanding of the Pali Canon) or a shunyata that cannot develop because it's not a thing (according to Mahayana).

Here we can benefit from Buddhist teachings about the "two truths," which distinguish the ultimate (absolute) truth from conventional (relative) truth. There are different ways to understand the distinction between them, but for present purposes it is helpful to focus on the difference between a shunyata perspective ("form is emptiness") and a form perspective ("emptiness is form"). Let's call them the vertical and the horizontal dimensions, respectively.

From the vertical perspective there is no such thing as evolutionary progress, because no matter how simple or complex phenomena (forms, things, processes, etc.) may be, they remain "empty" of any self-being. To say it yet again, everything is interdependent, arising and passing away according to conditions. In cosmological terms, the ceaseless generativity that *is* the self-organizing universe takes one form after another, according to the available possibilities. All of them are equivalent insofar as they are impermanent products of the same creative process. There is no progress or decline because shunyata has nothing to gain or lose. There is no more value to a rock or a tree than to gorilla or a human. We may not like it, but Gandhi is no better than Hitler, because better or worse does not apply. Each of them simply *is*, not as a distinct thing, but as a lacking-nothing manifestation of the cosmos. And it is important to appreciate that from this perspective nothing is lost if civilization as we know it collapses or even if humanity becomes extinct. The generativity of the universe will continue by taking other forms.

> The Tao sustains and nurtures all things
> without discrimination.
>
> —LAO-TSE

Yet there is also the horizontal ("emptiness is form") perspective, which has sometimes been underemphasized in the Buddhist tradition, for understandable reasons. Normally we are motivated to begin our practice because of some suffering—which usually means because of the discomfort that arises from attachment to some particular forms: physical, mental, or both. Naturally, then, there is initial emphasis on realizing the "emptiness" of such forms, but focusing only on this is one sided. To realize my "self-nature that is no-nature" (Hakuin) is to experience the generative source of the cosmos. Yet simply to dwell there, indifferent to what arises from (or within) that groundless ground, is a misunderstanding that "clings to emptiness." The point is not to rest serenely in the source but to be open for that which springs forth nondually from it—for example, not to get rid of all thoughts but to think more creatively, which can occur when "I" am not the one "doing" the thinking.

From this horizontal perspective we can and sometimes must distinguish between forms: Gandhi was better than Hitler. There is evolutionary progress—from unicellular to multicellular life, from reptilian to mammalian brains, from conscious primates to self-conscious human beings. And, so far as we know, only with or as humans can the cosmos wake up and become self-aware, as happened with Gautama Buddha.

Creatures that Create

> The universe has made beings who cultivate beings.
>
> —PAUL R. FLEISHMAN

So the "two truths" doctrine of Buddhism helps to answer the question of whether human beings are special in some way (which does not necessarily mean that we have dominion over the rest of creation) or no different than any other species (as Stephen Jay Gould and deep ecologists claim). It turns out that both perspectives are valid. Insofar as everything is equally shunya, we are creatures just like every other creature and of no more value. Each species can be considered an experiment of the biosphere, and according to biologists less than one percent of all the species that have ever appeared on earth still survive. Given what we are doing to the biosphere, it is by no means evident that our oversized brains will make us an exception to this general rule. Even if we extinguish ourselves, however, if it's important for the cosmos to become self-aware, then it is likely to develop other ways to do so.

Nevertheless, there is something that distinguishes human beings from other species. It is not merely that we are a way that the universe can become self-aware. We are not only creatures that know we are creatures: *we are creatures that create and know that we create*. If the cosmos *is* the creative process, we are its epicenters, in a way that none of its other forms are (so far as we know). With us, new types of creativity and flourishing become possible.

> To be human is to know what it feels like
> to be evolution happening.
> —TERRENCE DEACON

Many species create in one way or another. Male bowerbirds build elaborate nests to attract a mate. African termites construct complex mounds up to thirty feet high that include nursery chambers and fungal gardens. Unlike these instinctive behaviors, however, humans create something immeasurably more complex and interesting: culture, which in turn re-creates us and conditions the further possibilities we can envision and realize. If we don't assume the usual distinction between biological and cultural evolution, we can see civilization as a continuation of the same generative process. If "God" can be taken as a metaphor for this creative process, is this what being "made in the image of God" (Genesis 1:27) means? Our supersized neocortex and opposable thumb enable us to be co-creators.

> Our imaginative minds seem to be the planet's way
> of collecting and refracting this immense array
> of sentience and ways of being.
> —SUSAN MURPHY

We transform eating into growing food, cooking, and dining; procreation into romance, weddings, honeymoons, marriage, and family life (and divorce); communicative grunts into literature, philosophy, and other types of storytelling. We create new "species" that could never evolve without us: hand axes and knives, bridges and wells, houses and schools, temples and cathedrals, string quartets and jazz quartets, economic systems and political institutions, scientific research and technological development... In this fashion the cosmos, which we are a manifestation of, becomes infinitely richer in ever-ramifying possibilities.

> We have a mission to create, for we are evolution incarnate.
> We are her self-awareness, her frontal lobes and fingertips....
> We are parts of something 3.5 billion years old, but pubertal in
> cosmic time. We are neurons of this planet's interspecies mind.
> —HOWARD BLOOM, *Global Brain*

Our usual understanding of human creativity assumes that people, individually or collectively, are solely responsible for their creations. An artist paints a painting, a composer composes a musical score, a novelist writes a novel, and in each case what is created is their own product. In a self-organizing universe, however, that perspective becomes inadequate: if biological and cultural evolution are different aspects of the same creative process, humans are better understood as the means whereby the whole cosmos creates, for we are not self-sufficient causes. And many great creators have been aware of this. More than a few composers, for example, have confided that their greatest works were not composed by themselves: in a state of heightened receptivity they *heard* what they wrote down. It rises up through the bottom of the bucket, as it were. Stravinsky was explicit: "I heard, and I wrote what I heard. I am the vessel through which *The Rite of Spring* passed." Other descriptions use more nondual metaphors. Mozart referred to his musical invention as taking place in a "pleasing, lively dream" in which "my subject enlarges itself, becomes methodized and defined, and the whole, though it be long, stands almost complete and finished in my mind." Tchaikovsky's description is similar:

> Generally speaking, the germ of a future composition comes
> suddenly and unexpectedly.... It takes root with extraordi-
> nary force and rapidity, shoots up through the earth, puts

forth branches, leaves, and, finally, blossoms. I cannot define
the creative process in any other way than by this simile.

If we include the experience of poets and other writers, it would be
easy to multiply these examples a hundredfold. And if we take their
testimony seriously, it points to a source for human creativity that is
much deeper than the usual sense of self.

Modernity has brought about an explosion of creativity incomparably
more complex and sophisticated than anything that existed previously.
Today innovation of all sorts has become an ever-accelerating positive
feedback loop, as technological developments and other achievements
inspire new ones. Thanks to new communication media, only one person needs to discover something important; within a few days most
people who follow the news can know about it, and within a few years
it can be utilized around the world.

We have become so accustomed to this process that we now take it
for granted, yet it is one of the most extraordinary features of contemporary life. Although I am as concerned as anyone to decry the institutionalized greed that motivates and exploits so much economic activity
today, capitalism with its encouragement of the entrepreneurial spirit
has played an essential role in promoting that creativity, and continues
to do so—for better and worse.

The Meaning of It All

The more the universe seems comprehensible, the more it
also seems pointless.
—STEVEN WEINBERG, NOBEL LAUREATE IN PHYSICS

The most important thing that humans create is *meaning*. Because of
our distinctive ways of valuing and intending, it is with us (or, to express
it less dualistically: in us, as us) that the cosmos becomes meaningful
in a new way. To examine the universe objectively and conclude that

it is pointless misses the point. *Who* is comprehending that the universe is pointless? Someone separate from it, or someone who is an inextricable part of it? If cosmologists too are a manifestation of the same universe that cosmologists study, with them the universe is comprehending itself. Does that change the universe? When we come to see the universe in a new way, it's the universe that is coming to see itself in a new way.

Weinberg's bleak scientific conclusion is very different from the traditional mythologies of perhaps all premodern societies. For them the world is objectively meaningful in the sense that humans are a part of a larger pattern and that we have an important role to play in maintaining that order. As mentioned in part I, Mesopotamians believed that humans had been created by the gods as their slaves, to provide the temples and labor that were needed to appease and support them. In ancient Egypt, rituals were necessary to keep the sky goddess Nut separated from the earth god Geb; otherwise chaos would overwhelm the earth. Many pre-Columbian Mesoamerican societies believed that human sacrifices were necessary to sustain the cosmos, the most famous example being the Aztec practice of cutting out the still-beating hearts of war victims as offerings to Huitzilopochtli, the sun god.

Most of the world no longer believes in such problematic mythologies, yet belief that the universe is ultimately pointless is burdensome in a different fashion. In one way, meaning is inescapable; it is built into our priorities. If my focus is "looking out for number one," the meaning of my life becomes the promotion of my own best interests. If my own well-being cannot really be separated from the well-being of others, then that basic orientation may be based on a delusion, and if that delusion is widespread, the meaning built into the functioning of a whole society can be self-stultifying and even self-destructive. Such an orientation may nonetheless seem appropriate if the universe is pointless and our species is nothing more than an evolutionary accident. But if we are a way the generative cosmos becomes self-aware, there are more interesting possibilities.

> The more we know about our universe,
> the more difficult it becomes to believe in determinism.
> —ILYA PRIGOGINE, *The End of Certainty*

One important human characteristic, apparently unique, is that we can develop the ability to "dis-identify" from anything and everything, letting go not only of the individual sense of separate self but also of collective selves as well: dissociating from patriarchy (I'm a man not a woman), nationalism (I'm American not Chinese), racism (I'm white not black), even speciesism (I'm human, not a "lower animal"). Meditation encourages such nonattachment, of course, which is necessary to realize one's nondwelling mind. Yet the point of such letting go is not to dissociate from everything. It's just the opposite: by not taking this side rather than that, we become receptive to both. By not identifying with either, we can come to identify with everything.

> For one species to mourn the death of another is a new
> thing under the sun.... We, who have lost our [passenger]
> pigeons, mourn the loss. Had the funeral been ours,
> the pigeons would hardly have mourned us.
> —ALDO LEOPOLD

That human beings are the only species (so far as we know) that can *know* it is a manifestation of the entire cosmos opens up a possibility that may need to be embraced if we are to survive the crises that now confront us. *We can choose to work for the well-being of the whole,* to make that the meaning of our lives. "The well-being of the whole" in this case can mean not only the well-being of the biosphere, but conceivably even (should a suitable situation arise) for the well-being of the whole universe. That we are the self-awareness of the cosmos makes the whole cosmos our body, in effect, which implies not only a special understanding but also a special role in response to that realization. Is that the answer to the greatest problem of all: the meaning of human life, both individual and collective? And is that how the bodhisattva path should be understood today?

> Whatever living beings there be—feeble or strong, long, stout, or medium, short, small, or large, seen or unseen, dwelling far or near... may all beings be happy! Just as a mother would protect her only child even at the risk of her own life, even so, let one cultivate a boundless heart toward all beings. Let one's thoughts of boundless love pervade the whole world—above, below, and across—without any obstruction, without any hatred, without any enmity.
>
> —METTA SUTTA

If what Buddhism describes as "waking up" is how the universe becomes aware of itself, we are the species by which the universe becomes meaningful as a whole. Then to ask whether the universe itself is objectively meaningful or meaningless is to miss the point—as if the universe were outside us, or simply there without us. When we do not erase ourselves from the picture, we can see that we are meaning-makers, the beings by which the universe introduces a new scale of meaning and value.

> We—all intelligent, self-aware creatures that may exist in any galaxy—are the universe's only means of reflecting on and understanding itself. Together we are the self-consciousness of the universe. The entire universe is meaningless without us.
>
> —NANCY ELLEN ABRAMS AND JOEL E. PRIMACK

A Pivotal Stage

It's not going to be easy, of course. The other side of creativity is freedom, for without it there is only a mechanical exercise in cause and effect. We are free to derive the meaning of our lives from delusions about who we are—from dysfunctional stories about what the world is and how we fit into it—or we can derive that meaning from insight into our nonduality with the world. In either case, there are consequences.

The problem with basing one's life on delusions is that the consequences are unlikely to be good. As well as producing poetry and cathedrals, our ingenuity has recently found creative expression in world wars, concentration camps, and genocides, as well as the proliferation of nuclear bombs and other weapons of mass destruction, to mention only a few of the disagreeable examples that could be cited. We are in the early stages of an ecological crisis that threatens the natural and cultural legacy of future generations, including a mass extinction event that may lead to the disappearance of half the earth's plant and animal species by the end of this century, according to E. O. Wilson—an extinction event that may eventually include ourselves. What needs to be done so that our extraordinary co-creative powers will promote collective well-being (*collective* in this case referring to all the ecosystems of the biosphere)?

In Nietzsche's *Thus Spake Zarathustra* Zarathustra declares that "Man is a rope stretched between the animal and the Overman—a rope over an abyss.... What is great in man is that he is a bridge and not a goal." Are we transitional? Must we evolve further—not biologically but culturally—in order to survive at all?

> The fundamental immaturity of the human species
> at this time in history is that our systems of governance
> and economics not only permit but actually encourage
> subsets of the whole (individuals and corporations)
> to benefit at the expense of the whole.
> —MICHAEL DOWD, *Thank God for Evolution*

From a Buddhist perspective the basic problem is not so much moral as cognitive. Our unethical tendencies ultimately derive from a misapprehension: the delusion of a self that is separate from others. Insofar as we are ignorant of our true nature, individual and collective narcissism naturally motivates us to be self-centered.

In other words, the fundamental issue is not self-love but a profound misunderstanding of what one's self really is. Without the compassion that arises when we realize our nonduality—from empathy not only with other humans but with the whole of the biosphere—it is becoming not only possible but likely that civilization as we know it will not survive the next few centuries. Nor would it deserve to. Then is the eco-crisis a collective spiritual crisis? Is the earth challenging us to wake up or get out of the way? It remains to be seen whether the *Homo sapiens sapiens* experiment will continue to be a successful vehicle for the cosmic evolutionary process.

> Human beings have reached what may well be a pivotal stage
> in their evolution. They have been created by the universe,
> in the universe, as an integral part of the universe. They have passed
> through a difficult period when their strong day-to-day experience
> of selfhood and their cultural conditioning have made them feel
> detached from the reality in which they are permanently embedded.
> And now they are beginning to see beyond the self again
> into the truth of their conditioning.
> —DAVID DARLING, *Zen Physics*

Perhaps exemplars like the Buddha and Gandhi are harbingers, or prototypes, of how our species needs to develop. If so, the cultural development that is most needed today involves spiritual practices that address the fiction of a discrete self. Neurologists have discovered that contemplative practices can actually reconfigure the way the brain functions: during meditation the brain is rewiring itself. If my desire to awaken is, from a more nondual perspective, the urge of the universe itself to become self-aware, can we also say that it is the cosmic creative process that is rewiring its own brain?

> The Buddha attained individual awakening. Now we need
> a collective enlightenment to stop the course of destruction.
>
> —THICH NHAT HANH

TODAY WE ARE CHALLENGED to discover the meaning and role we seek in the ongoing, long-term task of repairing the rupture between us and mother earth. Will our species wake up to become the collective bodhisattva of the biosphere? Thich Nhat Hanh has recently suggested that the next buddha may appear as a sangha—as a community rather than as an avatar who will come to save us from ourselves. We must become that which we have been waiting for. In order for that to happen, we need this alternative story such as this one (or something similar) about what it means to be a human being today.

That's not to say that this new story is complete or finished—or that it ever will be. Buddhist emphasis on impermanence and insubstantiality applies to stories as well, including Buddhist ones, including this one. We don't just need stories, we need stories that are open to revision and self-correction. If stories are how we try to grasp the world once-and-for-all, their transience is as regrettable as our own. If our stories are a way that the universe is coming to understand itself, we can delight in being an ephemeral part of that process.

CHALLENGE

The mercy of the West has been social revolution.
The mercy of the East has been individual insight
into the basic self/void. We need both.

—GARY SNYDER, *Earth House Hold*

T O UNPACK Gary Snyder's insight: the highest ideal of the
Western tradition has been the concern to restructure
our societies so that they become more socially just.
The most important goal for Buddhism is to awaken and (to use the
Zen phrase) realize one's true nature, which puts an end to dukkha—
especially that associated with the delusion of a separate self. Today it
has become more obvious that we need both of these aspirations, not
just because these ideals complement each other, but because each
project needs the other.

The Western conception of justice largely originates with the Abrahamic traditions, particularly the Hebrew prophets, who fulminated
against oppressive rulers for afflicting the poor and powerless. Describing Old Testament prophecy, Walter Kaufmann writes that "no other
sacred scripture contains books that speak out against social injustice
as eloquently, unequivocally, and sensitively as the books of Moses and
some of the prophets." Is there a Buddhist equivalent? Although the
doctrine of karma understands something like justice as an impersonal
moral law built into the fabric of the cosmos, historically karma has

functioned differently from the Abrahamic version. Combined with the doctrine of rebirth (a corollary, since evil people sometimes prosper in this life) and the belief that each of us is now experiencing the consequences of actions in previous lifetimes, the implication seems to be that we do not need to be concerned about pursuing justice, because sooner or later everyone gets what they deserve. In practice, this has often encouraged passivity and acceptance of one's situation, rather than a commitment to promote social justice.

Does the Buddhist emphasis on dukkha provide a better parallel with the Western conception of justice? Dukkha is unquestionably Buddhism's most important concept: according to the Pali Canon, Gautama Buddha said that what he had to teach was dukkha and how to end it. The best-known summary of the Buddha's teachings, the four Noble Truths, is all about dukkha, its cause, its extinction, and how to extinguish it. Historically, Asian Buddhism has focused on individual dukkha and personal karma, a limitation that may have been necessary in autocratic polities that could and sometimes did repress Buddhist institutions. Today, however, the globalization of democracy, human rights, and freedom of speech opens the door to new ways of responding to social causes of dukkha, and a more socially engaged Buddhism has been developing.

On the other side, the Abrahamic emphasis on justice, in combination with the classical Greek realization that society is a collective construct that can be restructured, has resulted in our modern concern to reform political and economic institutions. This has involved, most obviously, a variety of human rights movements. As valuable as these social reforms have been, as much as they have achieved, the limitations of such an institutional approach, by itself, are becoming evident. Even the best possible economic and political system cannot be expected to function well if the people within that system remain motivated by greed, aggression, and delusion—the "three fires" or "three poisons" that Buddhism encourages us to transform into their more positive counterparts: generosity, loving-kindness, and wisdom.

Today, in our globalizing world, the modern Western focus on social transformation encounters the traditional Buddhist focus on individual awakening. Their encounter helps us understand why each has had limited success, and challenges us with new possibilities. We need to see why they need each other in order to actualize their own ideals. Some of the implications of that interdependence will be explored by looking at our present economic and ecological situation from a Buddhist as well as a Western perspective.

Good vs. Evil

The Abrahamic religions emphasize, most of all, morality. God's main way of relating to us, his creatures, is instructing us how to live by giving us ethical commandments. To be a good Jew, Christian, or Muslim is to follow those rules. The fundamental axis is *good vs. evil*: doing what God wants us to do (in which case we will be rewarded) and not doing what he does not want us to do (to avoid punishment). According to one common version, this world is a battleground where God and Satan contend with each other, and where the most important issue is whose side you are on.

Even the supposed origin of human history—the Genesis story of Adam and Eve—is understood as an act of disobedience against God the Father. Earlier I mentioned that the story can also be taken as a myth about the development of self-consciousness (and its shadow, a sense of lack), but the focus is explicitly on the moral dimension. According to some Christian accounts, we still suffer due to the original sin of our primal parents.

Later, because of the wickedness and corruption of the human race— in other words, people were not living the way God wanted them to— God sends a great flood that drowns all humans and animals except those in Noah's ark. Eventually God formalizes his moral instructions to humanity with a covenant that includes giving the Ten Commandments to Moses. Jesus has a more intimate relationship with God the

Father and emphasizes that we should love one another, yet this does not abrogate the importance of living according to God's commands: of our will submitting to his will.

Although many people in the modern world no longer believe in an Abrahamic God, morality—the struggle between good and evil—arguably remains our favorite story. It is the main theme in most popular novels, films, and television shows (think of James Bond, Star Wars, Harry Potter, not to mention every detective novel and TV crime series). From a Buddhist perspective, however, this preoccupation with good vs. evil is…well, both good and evil: there's something wonderful about it, but also something very problematic. Let's start with the problem.

> "There is no good and evil, there is only power,
> and those too weak to seek it."
> —LORD VOLDEMORT

The duality between good and evil is a prime example of the difficulty that often occurs with dualistic concepts, when we think in terms of bipolar opposites such as high and low, big and small, light and dark, etc. Although those particular examples are usually innocuous, other instances are more problematical because we want one pole and not the other. Yet, because the meaning of each is the opposite of the other (we do not really know what "high" means unless we know what "low" means), we cannot have one without the other. Although this point may seem quite abstract, it's true not only logically but also psychologically. If, for example, it is really important for you to live a *pure* life (however you understand purity), you will inevitably be preoccupied with (avoiding) *impurity*.

> Genuine purity of mind is a state beyond purity and impurity.
> —CHAN MASTER HUI HAI

The relationship between good and evil may be the most problematical example of dualistic thinking, because their interdependence means that we do not know what good is until we determine what evil is (good requires avoiding evil) and that we feel good about ourselves when we are struggling against that evil—an evil *outside* ourselves, of course. Hence inquisitions, witchcraft and heresy trials, and, most recently, the War on Terror. What was the difference between Osama bin Laden and George W. Bush? They were not only polar opposites but mirror images of each other: both fighting the same holy war of Good against Evil, each leading the forces of goodness in a struggle against the forces of evil, because that is what the forces of good are supposed to do. Once something has been identified as evil, there is no need to understand it or accommodate it; our task is to destroy it.

> You're either with us or against us.
> —GEORGE W. BUSH

The War on Terror illustrates the tragic paradox: historically, one of the main causes of evil has been our attempts to destroy evil, or what we have understood as evil. What was Hitler trying to do? Eliminate the evil elements that pollute the world: Jews, homosexuals, Roma gypsies, and so forth. Stalin attempted to do the same with landowning peasants, as did Mao Zedong with Chinese landlords. Lest one conclude that this is a fascist and communist problem, we should also remember the 1965–66 massacre of up to a million "leftists" by the Suharto regime in Indonesia—with the covert assistance of the U.S. government.

> It's not enough to hate your enemy. You have to understand
> how the two of you bring each other to deep completion.
> —DON DELILLO, *Underworld*

There is, however, also a very positive side to the duality between good and evil, which brings us back to the Hebrew prophets. One of the earliest, Amos, castigates those who "trample the head of the poor into the dust of the earth" and "crush the needy"; prayers and sacrifices cannot make up for such evil deeds. Isaiah complains about those "who write oppressive laws, to turn aside the needy from justice and to rob the poor of my people of their right, that widows may be your spoil, and that you may make the orphans your prey." Both speak on behalf of God, and both address themselves primarily to rulers who abuse their power. Of course many more examples could be cited from the Bible: speaking truth to power, the prophets called for social justice for the oppressed, who suffer from what might be called *social* dukkha.

THE OTHER SOURCE of modern Western civilization is classical Greece, which discovered the momentous distinction between *physis* (the natural world) and *nomos* (social convention). In effect, this was the realization that *whatever is socially constructed can be reconstructed*: we can reorganize our own societies and in that way (attempt to) determine our own collective destiny. This was another important aspect of the Axial revolution that occurred in the middle of the first millennium BCE. The Axial Age took form as new religions in India, China, and the Middle East, but in Greece it inspired the beginnings of philosophy, science, and this new perspective on how we live together.

As mentioned earlier, pre-Axial Age cultures such as the Mesopotamians, Egyptians, and Aztecs generally assumed that their hierarchical social structures were as "natural" as their local ecosystems. We consider the Greeks *humanists* because their discovery about social convention challenged the archaic religious worldview that embedded the traditional political order within the larger natural order of things. Now humans could consciously determine for themselves how to live together.

An unusual set of cultural conditions encouraged this development. Consistent with Homer's detached, ironical attitude toward the gods, most of the Greek city-states had no sacred scripture or powerful priesthood. Their merchant fleets sparked a great colonizing movement that exposed the Greeks to very different cultures, which encouraged relativism and skepticism toward their own myths. And unlike Moses and Mohammed, Solon did not get his tablets from a deity when he gave Athens new laws.

With the help of some remarkable leaders, Athens was able to reorganize itself more or less peacefully. Cleisthenes replaced the four traditional, family-based tribes of Athens with ten districts, supplanting kinship identity with one's area of residence. Pericles extended the access of humble citizens to public office. The result was a provocative experiment in direct democracy, although a very limited one by today's standards—women and slaves did not qualify.

Not everyone liked democracy. Plato never forgot what happened to Socrates, and offered more elitist plans to restructure the Greek city-state in two of his dialogues, the *Republic* and the *Laws*. Such alternative visions nevertheless presupposed the same distinction between *physis* and *nomos*. The various revolutions that for better and worse have reconstructed our modern world—English, American, French, Russian, Chinese, etc.—all took for granted such an understanding: if a political regime is unjust and oppressive, it should be challenged, because social structures are collective human creations that can be recreated.

Bringing together the Hebrew concern for social justice with the Greek realization that society can be restructured has resulted in the highest ideal of the modern West, actualized in reform and revolutionary movements, democratic government, human rights, etc.—in short, social progress. We are all too aware of the shortcomings of this progress, but our concern with those shortcomings itself testifies to our social justice principles, which we understand to be universal but are nonetheless historically conditioned and not to be taken for granted.

Of course, even with the best ideals (what might be called our "collective intentions"), our societies have not become as socially just as most of us would like, and in some ways they are becoming more unjust. An obvious economic example is the gap between rich and poor in the United States, and in much of the rest of the world as well, a disparity that is not only obscenely large but increasing. How shall we understand this discrepancy between ideal and reality? One obvious reply is that our economic system, as it presently operates, is still unjust because wealthy people and powerful corporations manipulate our political systems, for their own self-centered and short-sighted benefit. So we need to keep working for a more equitable economic system, and for a democratic process free of such distortions.

I would not challenge that explanation, but by itself is it sufficient? Is the basic difficulty that our economic and political institutions are not structured well enough to avoid such manipulations, or might it be the case that they *cannot* be structured well enough—in other words, that we cannot rely only on an institutional solution to structural injustice? Is it possible to create a social order so perfect that it will function well regardless of the personal motivations of the people so ordered, or do we also need to find ways to address those motivations?

The Greek experiment with democracy failed for the same reasons that our modern experiment with democracy is in danger of failing: unless social reconstruction is accompanied by personal reconstruction, democracy merely empowers the ego-self. Insofar as I am still motivated by greed, ill will, and delusion, my freedom is likely to make things worse. So long as the illusion of a discrete self, separate from others, prevails, democracy simply provides different types of opportunities for individuals to take advantage of other individuals.

Athenians became aware of this problem quite early. According to Herbert Muller's *Freedom in the Ancient World*, Greek individualism "was rooted in the Homeric tradition of personal fame and glory and was nourished by habitual competition, as much in art and athletics as in business, but everywhere off the battlefield with little team play." This individualism "was tempered by little sense of strictly moral responsibility, or in particular of altruism." It soon became obvious that private appetites were corrupting the democratic process. Demosthenes lamented that politics had become the path to riches, for individuals no longer placed the state before themselves but viewed it as another way to promote their own personal advantage. Plato's *Republic* argues that the democratic personality fails because it lacks a coherent organizing principle and yields to the strongest pressures of the moment—a recipe for interpersonal as well as intrapersonal strife.

Sound familiar? Perhaps this also helps us to understand why so many political revolutions have ended so badly, with one gang of thugs replaced by a different gang of thugs. Suppose, for example, that I am a revolutionary leader who successfully overthrows an oppressive regime. If I have not also worked on transforming my own motivations—my greed, aggression, and delusion—I will be sorely tempted to take personal advantage of my new situation, inclined to see those who disagree with me as enemies to be purged, and (the number-one ego problem?) disposed to see the solution to social problems in my superior judgment and the imposition of my decisions. Unsurprisingly, such motivations are unlikely to result in a society that is truly just. And the history of Athens reminds us—as if we need to be reminded—that these distortions are not confined only to authoritarian rulers.

If we can never have a social structure so good that it obviates the need for people to be good (in Buddhist terms, to make efforts not to be motivated by greed, aggression, and delusion), then our modern emphasis on social transformation—restructuring institutions to make them more just—is necessary but not adequate by itself. That brings us to the Buddhist focus on personal transformation.

Ignorance vs. Awakening

> As human beings, our greatness lies not so much in being able to remake the world—that is the myth of the atomic age—as in being able to remake ourselves.
>
> —MAHATMA GANDHI

Of course, ethical behavior is also important in Buddhism. Laypeople are expected to follow the five precepts (to avoid harming living beings, taking what is not given, sexual misconduct, improper speech, and intoxicants), and hundreds of additional rules and regulations are prescribed for monastics. But if we view them in an Abrahamic fashion we are liable to miss the main point. Since there is no Buddhist God telling us that we must live this way, the precepts are important because living in accordance with them means that the circumstances and quality of our own lives will naturally improve. They can be understood as exercises in mindfulness—vows to train ourselves in certain ways.

The precepts can be compared to the training wheels on the bicycle of a young child, which can be removed as the child learns how to ride. In the Brahmajala Sutta—one of the most important Pali suttas, in fact the first sutta in the Digha Nikaya—the Buddha distinguishes between what he calls "elementary, inferior matters of moral practice" and "other matters, profound, hard to see, hard to understand... experienced by the wise" that he has realized.

He makes that distinction because for Buddhism the fundamental axis is not between good and evil but between ignorance/delusion and awakening/wisdom. The primary challenge is cognitive in the broad sense: becoming more aware of the way things really are. In principle, at least, someone who has awakened to the true nature of the world (including the true nature of oneself) no longer needs to follow an external moral code because he or she *naturally* wants to behave in a way that does not violate the spirit of the precepts. (The fact that, in practice, there have been so many cases of improper behavior by so-called enlightened teachers raises issues that are too complex to be pursued here.)

The Buddha emphasized that what he had to teach was dukkha and how to end it. Did he have in mind only individual dukkha, or did he have a wider social vision that encompassed structural dukkha: the suffering inflicted on many people by oppressive rulers and other unjust social arrangements? In *The Buddha: Buddhist Civilization in India and Ceylon*, the British scholar Trevor Ling argued that religions as we know them today are "reduced civilizations"—the remnants of movements originally much more ambitious:

> To say that Gotama the Buddha founded a religion is to prejudice our understanding of his far-reaching influence. For in modern usage the word religion denotes merely one department of human activity, now regarded of less and less public

importance, and belonging almost entirely to the realm of men's private affairs. But whatever else Buddhism is or is not, in Asia it is a great social and cultural tradition.

Ling believes that the Buddha intended to start a movement that would transform society, rather than merely establish a monastic order with alternative values to the mainstream. Certainly his attitudes toward women and caste were extraordinarily progressive for his day— more progressive than many of his followers, even today.

Earlier I discussed a controversial account in the Pali Canon of how the Buddha reluctantly agreed to establish a *bhikkhuni* sangha for nuns. It is evident that the version we read has been altered, to cast some doubt on the Buddha's decision ("It's Ananda's fault!") and to assert male control over women monastics. Despite many stories in the Pali Canon of bhikkhunis attaining various levels of enlightenment, including the highest, the bhikkhuni sangha apparently did not receive the same level of support as the male bhikkhu sangha, and it eventually disappeared. My guess is that some bhikkhus did not appreciate the competition.

Another incident in the Pali Canon gives insight into the Buddha's attitude toward the caste system, which during his time was not as rigid as it became afterward, yet even then was a considerable source of social dukkha. According to the Vinaya account, six young high-caste men, whose barber was Upali, decided to join the Buddhist sangha. They gave their elegant robes and ornaments to him with instructions to bring them back home, but Upali was worried that he might be accused of stealing them. So he decided to join the sangha as well. One version of the story is that the high-caste applicants then asked the Buddha to ordain Upali first. According to another version the Buddha decided to test the high-caste men before ordaining them, by sending them on a meditation retreat; while they were so engaged he ordained Upali. Since seniority in the sangha is determined by when one joins, that meant he would always be senior to the other six.

In either case, the point is important: within the sangha there is no discrimination on the basis of caste. Trevor Ling has called the sangha the first democratic institution in history. It suggests that the Buddha did not support the caste system, although any broader social implications of that are more difficult to infer.

Ling reminds us of something else that is easy to overlook. Among academics in the field of religious studies, the very concept of "religion" is contested; no definition has ever become generally accepted. Our usual experience of religion today—going to church on Sunday morning is the classic example—is very different from the more central role of religion in the premodern West and from its greater role in many nonmodern cultures even today. As mentioned previously, everyday life in medieval Europe was saturated with religious activities: daily prayers, mass and other sacraments, processions, public penances and pilgrimages, the yearly calendar of holy days, and so forth. This suggests that we should not anachronistically project our enervated contemporary understanding of religion back onto the life and times of the Buddha. It also complicates the familiar question about whether or not Buddhism is a religion: what we think of as "religion" must be quite different from what it meant to the Buddha and his contemporaries. Given the paucity of historical documents, however, we may never know what the Buddha hoped for the larger social influence of the sangha.

Regardless of what Gautama Buddha may or may not have intended, what apparently happened after his *parinibbana* is that within a few generations much of the sangha settled down in places that became monasteries. Some bhikkhus continued to practice in the forest but not much is known about them. Early Buddhism as an institution came to an accommodation with the state, relying not only on the tolerance of kings and emperors but also their material support to some extent. And if you want to be supported by the powers-that-be, you'd better support the powers-that-be. Because no Asian Buddhist society was democratic, that placed limits on what types of dukkha Buddhist teachers could emphasize.

Is that how Buddhism became "reduced" to a religion? The tradition as it developed could not address structural dukkha—for example, the exploitative policies of many rulers—that ultimately could only be resolved by some institutional transformation. On the contrary, the karma-and-rebirth teaching could easily be used—and was—to legitimate the power of kings and princes, who must be reaping the fruits of their benevolent actions in past lifetimes, and to rationalize the disempowerment of those born poor or disabled, who must also be experiencing the consequences of (unskillful) actions in previous lifetimes.

We in the West take for granted the principle of separation between church and state, but that distinction is another modern concept. Asian Buddhist rulers were not only patrons and defenders of the sangha; they also served as cultural idealizations and living symbols of the social order, necessary to maintain harmony between the state and the cosmos. In other words, their role was religious as well as political. Today we see this as an example of collective mystification, yet it has been the norm in Buddhist cultures and was common in the West's not-too-distant past (for instance, "the divine right of kings" of medieval Europe). Chinese emperors claimed to be bodhisattvas and even buddhas, and understandably few dared to contradict them. Perhaps we still see vestiges today in the attitude of many Thai people toward their king, and in the reverence of many Tibetans for their Dalai Lama, until very recently a "god-king."

The coming of Buddhism to the West—more precisely, the globalization of Buddhism—challenges such mystifications, even as modern Europe long ago overthrew its absolute monarchs. Secularism and democracy are liberating Buddhism from any need to cozy up to autocratic rulers. In most locales Buddhists and Buddhist institutions are no longer subject to oppressive polities, and we also have a much better understanding of the structural causes of dukkha. This opens the door to expanded possibilities for the tradition, which can now develop more freely the social implications of its basic perspective. As Buddhist emphasis on impermanence and insubstantiality suggests, history need not be destiny.

Another way to express the relationship between the Western ideal of social transformation (that is, social justice that addresses social dukkha) and the Buddhist goal of personal transformation (an awakening that addresses individual dukkha) is in terms of different types of freedom. The emphasis of the modern West has been on individual freedom from oppressive institutions, a prime example being the Bill of Rights appended to the U.S. Constitution. The emphasis of Buddhism (and some other Asian traditions) has been on what might be called *psycho-spiritual* freedom. Freedom for the self, or freedom from the self? Today we can see more clearly the limitations of each freedom by itself. What have I gained if I am free from external control but still at the mercy of my own greed, aggression, and delusions? And awakening from the delusion of a separate self will not by itself free me, or all those with whom I remain interdependent, from the dukkha perpetuated by an exploitative economic system and an oppressive government. Again, we need to actualize both ideals to be truly free.

One might conclude from this that contemporary Buddhism simply needs to incorporate a Western concern for social justice. Yet that would overlook the distinctive implications of the Buddhist understanding of dukkha, craving, and delusion. To draw out some of those implications, the next sections offer a Buddhist perspective on our economic and ecological situations today. They summarize arguments I have made elsewhere, but it is important to see their relevance in this context.

The Economic Challenge

Until the modern era, economic theory was understood to be part of social philosophy, and in principle at least subordinate to religious authority (e.g., Church prohibitions of "usury"). Today the academic profession of economics is concerned to model itself on the authority of the hard sciences and become a "social science" by discovering the fundamental laws of economic exchange and development, which it hopes might be as objectively true as Newton's laws of motion.

In practice, such a focus tends to rationalize the kind of economy we have today, including the increasing gap between rich and poor. Despite many optimistic reports about economic recovery—for banks and investors, at least—in the U.S. that disparity continues to widen. At the time of writing, wealth is now the most concentrated it has been since 1916. We have become familiar with news reports that, for instance, the richest 400 families in America now have the same total wealth as the poorest half of Americans—over 150 million people. If, however, this is happening in accordance with the basic laws of economic science—well, we may not like this development and may try to constrain it in some way, but fundamentally we need to adapt to big disproportions. In this way such a disparity is "normalized," with the insinuation that it should be accepted.

"But it's not *fair!*" In opposition to such efforts to justify the present economic order, popular movements call for social justice—in this case, for distributive justice. Why should a wealthy few have so much and the rest of us so little? It is not difficult to imagine what the Hebrew prophets might say about this situation. For an economic system to be just, its benefits should be distributed much more equitably. And I would not disagree with that. But does the Buddhist emphasis on delusion-vs.-awakening provide an alternative perspective to supplement this concern for distributive justice?

Two implications of Buddhist teachings stand out here. One of them focuses on our individual predicament—one's personal role in our economic system—and the other implication considers the structural or institutional aspect of that system.

The first part of this book emphasized what I believe to be the single most important teaching of the Buddha: the relationship between duk-kha "suffering" and *anatta* "nonself." In contemporary terms, one's sense of self is a psychological and social construction that does not have any *svabhava* "self-existence" of its own. Being composed of mostly habitual ways of thinking, feeling, acting, intending, remembering, and so forth—processes that are impermanent and insubstantial—such a construct is inevitably haunted by dukkha: inherently insecure, because not only ungrounded but ungroundable.

As explained earlier, we commonly experience this as the feeling that something is wrong with me, that something is missing or not quite right about my life. In other words, an unawakened sense of self is haunted by a sense of *lack*. Usually, however, we misunderstand the source of our discomfort and believe that what we are lacking is something outside ourselves. And this brings us back to our individual economic predicament, because in the "overdeveloped" world we often grow up conditioned to understand ourselves as consumers, and to understand the basic problem of our lives as getting more money in order to acquire more things, because they are what will eventually make us happy.

There is an almost perfect fit between this fundamental sense of *lack* that unenlightened beings have, according to Buddhism, and our present economic system, which uses advertising and other devices to persuade us that the next thing we buy will make us happy—which it never does, at least not for long. In other words, a consumerist economy exploits our sense of lack, instead of helping us understand and address the root problem. The system generates profits by perpetuating our discontent in a way that aggravates it and leaves us wanting more.

> The American dream has become the world's nightmare.
> —THICH NHAT HANH

Such a critique of consumerism is consistent with some recent studies by psychologists, sociologists, and even economists, who have discovered that once one attains a certain minimum income—a basic level of food and shelter—happiness does not increase in step with increasing wealth or consumerism. Rather, the most important determinant of how happy people are turns out to be the quality of one's relationships with other people. I suspect that the Buddha would not be surprised.

Notice that this Buddhist perspective does not mention distributive justice or any other type of social justice, nor does it offer an ethical evaluation. The basic problem is delusion rather than injustice or immorality. Yet this approach does not deny the inequities of our economic system, nor is it inconsistent with an Abrahamic ethical critique. Although an alternative viewpoint has been added, the ideal of social justice remains very important.

What does this imply about our economic institutions, the structural aspect? The Buddha had little to say about evil *per se*, but he had a lot to say about the three "roots of evil": greed, aggression, and delusion. When what I do is motivated by any of these three (and they tend to overlap), I create problems for myself (and often for others too, of course). Yet we not only have individual senses of self, we also have collective selves: I am a man not a woman, an American not a Chinese, and so forth. Do the problems with the three poisons apply to collective selves as well? To further complicate the issue, we also have much more powerful institutions than in the Buddha's time. These constitute another type of collective self that often assumes a life of its own, in the sense that such institutions have their own motivations built into them. Elsewhere I have argued that our present economic system can be understood as institutionalized greed; that our militarism institutionalizes aggression; and that the mainstream media institutionalize delusion, because their primary focus is profiting from advertising and consumerism, rather than educating or informing us about what is really happening.

If greed, aggression and delusion are the main sources of evil, and if today they have been institutionalized... well, you can draw your own conclusions. Here let's consider only the first poison: how our economic system promotes structural dukkha by institutionalizing greed.

One definition of greed is "never enough," something that does not function only personally: corporations are never large enough or profitable enough, the value of their shares is never high enough, our national GDP is never big enough.... In fact, we cannot imagine what "big enough" might be. It is built into these systems that they must keep growing, or else they tend to collapse.

Consider, in particular, the stock market, high temple of the economic process. On the one side are many millions of investors, most anonymous and mostly unconcerned about the activities of the corporations they invest in, except for their profitability and its effects on share prices. In many cases investors do not even know where their money is invested, thanks to mutual funds. Such an attitude is not disreputable, of course: on the contrary, investment is a highly respectable endeavor, and the most successful investors are idolized (Warren Buffet, "the sage of Omaha").

On the other side of the stock market, however, the desires and expectations of those millions of investors become transformed into an impersonal and unremitting pressure for growth and increased profitability that every CEO must respond to, and preferably in the short run. Contemplate, as an unlikely example, the CEO of a large transnational corporation, who one morning wakes up to the imminent dangers of climate change and wants to do everything he (it is usually a he) can to address this challenge. If what he tries to do threatens corporate profits, however, he is likely to lose his job. And if that is true for the CEO, how much more true it is for everyone else further down the corporate hierarchy. Corporations are legally chartered so that their first responsibility is not to their employees or customers, nor to other members of the societies they are part of, nor to the ecosystems of the earth, but to those who own them, who with very few exceptions are concerned primarily about return on investment—a preoccupation, again, that is not only socially acceptable but often lauded.

Who is responsible for this collective fixation on growth? The important point is that the system has attained not only a life of its own but its own motivations, quite apart from the motivations of the individuals who work for it and who will be replaced if they do not serve those institutional motivations. And all of us participate in this process in one way or another, as workers, consumers, investors, pensioners, and so forth, usually with little if any sense of personal responsibility for the collective result. Any awareness of what is actually happening tends to be diffused in the impersonal anonymity of this economic process. Everyone is just doing their job, playing their role.

In short, any genuine solution to the economic crisis will require more than some redistribution of wealth, necessary as that is, and it is not enough to append a concern for social justice to Buddhist teachings. Applying a Buddhist perspective to structural dukkha implies an alternative evaluation of our economic situation, which focuses on the consequences of individual and institutionalized delusion: the dukkha of a sense of a self that feels separate from others, whose sense of *lack* consumerism exploits and institutionalizes into economic structures that assume a life of their own. Although distributive justice remains important, in terms of equal opportunity and more equitable distribution, we must also find ways to address the personal dukkha built into consumerism and the structural dukkha built into institutions that have their own motivations. It has become obvious that what is beneficial for those institutions (in the short run) is very different from what is beneficial for the rest of us and for the earth's ecosystems.

> There's good news, and there's bad news.
> The bad news: civilization, as we know it, is about to end.
> Now, the good news: civilization, as we know it, is about to end.
> —SWAMI BEYONDANANDA

The Ecological Challenge

Does the basic Buddhist insight about the dukkha inherent to a (sense of) separate self also apply to our biggest collective sense of self: the duality between us as a species, *Homo sapiens sapiens*, and the rest of the biosphere?

The Buddha, like his contemporaries, knew nothing about climate change, carbon dioxide levels in the atmosphere, and so forth, yet he knew a lot about the delusion of self and the difficulties that gets us into. In fact, there seem to be precise and profound parallels between our usual individual predicament, as discussed earlier, and the present situation of human civilization. The basic problem in both cases is an uncomfortable sense of separation, our misunderstanding of the predicament, and our inappropriate reactions, which often aggravate the difficulty.

For this particular correspondence between individual and collective selves to hold, our collective sense of estrangement from the natural world must also be a source of collective frustration. And our collective response to that alienation—attempting to secure or "self-ground" ourselves technologically and economically—must be making things worse.

I mentioned earlier the important distinction that classical Greece made between *nomos* and *physis*, between the conventions of human society (governance, culture, technology, etc.) and the ecosystems of the natural world. Although today we take that insight for granted, it's not something that pre-Axial societies understood; they usually accepted their own social structures as inevitable because those structures were understood to be just as "natural" as their ecosystems.

This justified social hierarchies unacceptable today, yet there was nevertheless a psychological benefit in thinking that way: such societies shared a collective sense of meaning that the modern world has lost. For them, the meaning of their lives was built into the cosmos and revealed by their religion, which they took for granted. We, however, lack that kind of "social security," which is the basic psychological comfort that comes from knowing one's place and role in the world. The price of our freedom has been an increasing anxiety about who we are and what it means to be human.

There is a tension between such freedom (we decide what to value and do) and security (being grounded in something greater, which is taking care of us). Thanks to ever-more powerful technologies, it seems like we can accomplish almost anything we want to do, yet we don't know what we *should* want to do. What sort of world do we want to live in? What kind of society should we have? In this fashion too, our collective as well as individual lack of grounding in anything greater than ourselves has become a constant source of dukkha—an existential anxiety rooted in our sense of alienation from the natural world.

What has been our collective response to this predicament? Let's first remember how we usually react to our individual predicament: misunderstanding its source in the delusion of self, we look outside ourselves and become preoccupied with acquiring external things such as money, fame, and power. There is a collective parallel in our taken-for-granted obsession with never-ending economic growth and technological development. When will our GNP be large enough? When will have all the technology we need? Perhaps the word "progress" is misleading, because of course one can never have enough progress if it really is progress. Yet why is *more* always *better* if it can never be *enough*?

The important point is that economic growth and technological advances may be good *means* to accomplish something but they become problematical as *ends* in themselves. Insofar as we are not sure what we collectively want to do, however, they have become a collective substitute: we have become obsessed with ever-increasing power and control.

Notice the parallel with our individual predicament, according to Buddhism. Lacking the security that comes from knowing our place and role in the cosmos, we have been trying to create our own security by controlling the conditions of our existence, until everything becomes subject to our will, a "resource" that we can use. Ironically, if predictably, this has not been providing the sense of meaning and security that we seek. We have become more anxious, not less.

That project makes an ecological crisis inevitable, sooner or later. And if our reliance on technology as the solution to life's problems is itself a symptom of this larger problem, then the ecological crisis requires something more than a technological response (although technological developments such as more efficient solar panels are certainly necessary). Increasing dependence on ever-more sophisticated technologies can aggravate our sense of separation from the natural world, whereas any successful solution (if the parallel still holds) must include recognizing that we are an integral part of the natural world. That also means embracing our responsibility for the health of the whole biosphere, because its well-being ultimately cannot be distinguished from our own well-being.

If these parallels are helpful, they clarify what many have been intuiting: the ecological crisis is also a spiritual crisis. Just as the Buddhist perspective on our economic situation cannot be subsumed into the familiar social justice paradigm, so a Buddhist perspective on the ecological crisis requires something more than the usual preoccupation with trying to make industrial-growth society more "sustainable."

To sum up, we cannot expect either the economic or the ecological transformations we need to succeed without personal transformation as well, and the history of Buddhism shows that the opposite is also true: teachings that promote individual awakening cannot avoid being affected by social structures that promote collective delusion and craving. As the sociological paradox puts it, people create society, yet society also creates people.

Modern attempts at collective social reconstruction have had limited success because they tend to be compromised by ego-driven individual motivations. Buddhism and other nondualist traditions have also had limited success at eliminating dukkha and delusion, because they have been unable to challenge the dukkha and delusion built into oppressive social hierarchies that mystify themselves as necessary and beneficial. The convergence of those two projects in our times opens up fresh possibilities. They need each other. Or more precisely, we need both.

May each find in the other the supplementary perspective it needs to actualize its own deepest aspirations.

The New Bodhisattva

> Bodhisattva (Sanskrit, from bodhi "awakened" + sattva "being"): any person who, motivated by compassion, wishes to attain Buddhahood for the sake of all living beings.

The Western (now worldwide) ideal of a social transformation that institutionalizes social justice and ecological sustainability has achieved much, but not as much as we want or need. In fact, the more we learn about our situation, the more overwhelmed and discouraged many of us become. Climate breakdown... a mass extinction of species...

a dysfunctional economic system... corporate domination of government... overpopulation... This is a critical time in human history, and the collective decisions to be made during the next few years may set the course of events for many generations to come. The problems are so enormous and intimidating—where to start? We often end up feeling powerless, even paralyzed.

For those inspired by Buddhist teachings, an important issue is how much Buddhism can help us respond to these crises. This book has explored the relevance of Buddhist teachings to our present situation, but it's not enough to elaborate on those teachings: they require practice. We also seek examples of engagement that actually address the formidable challenges that face us.

Of course, we cannot expect to find precise answers to contemporary difficulties in ancient Buddhist texts. The Buddha lived in Iron Age India, and his society faced a different set of problems: for instance, aggressive monarchies competing to swallow up smaller states. Traditional Buddhism cannot help us decide whether to rein in growth-obsessed capitalism or to replace it with a more socially responsible economic system. We cannot depend on the Buddha to advise us whether a revitalized representative democracy can work well enough or whether we should push for more local, decentralized governance.

Nor does Buddhism imply a new political party or social movement, in my opinion. As Paul Hawken points out in *Blessed Unrest*, there are already a vast number of large and small organizations working for peace, social justice, and sustainability—well over two million, he now estimates. This encouraging number indicates a change of consciousness that is certainly not limited to Buddhist practitioners. The issue is whether a Buddhist perspective has something distinctive and pragmatic to offer, which can contribute something otherwise lacking in this movement. What might that be?

Historically, churches and churchgoers have played an important part in many Western reform movements—for example, in antislavery and civil rights campaigns. Nevertheless, much of the impetus in the West for deep structural change originates from socialism and other leftist movements, which traditionally have been suspicious of religion. Marx viewed religion as "the opiate of the people" because religious institutions have often been complicit with political oppression, using their doctrines to rationalize the authority of exploitative rulers and diverting believers' attention from their present condition to "the life to come." As we have noticed, this historical critique applies to some Buddhist institutions as well, yet a main concern of this book has been to demonstrate that at its best Buddhism offers an alternative approach: the path is really about personal transformation, about deconstructing and reconstructing the sense of self, not to qualify for a blissful afterlife but to live in a different way here and now.

Is there something specific within the Buddhist tradition that brings together personal and social transformation, in a new model of activism connecting inner and outer practice?

Yes: the bodhisattva.

In the Pali Canon, the bodhisattva refers to the earlier lives of Gautama Buddha before he became the Buddha. As Buddhism developed, however, the concept became a sectarian and divisive issue. According to one account, there was a conspicuous difference between the Buddha's accomplishment and that of the arahants who awakened by following his teaching. By definition, an arahant has attained the same awakening as the Buddha himself, yet the Buddha was nonetheless observed to be special because he so wholeheartedly devoted himself to helping everyone awaken. This perception led to the development of a more altruistic model of practice, which supposedly demonstrates the superiority of the Mahayana "Greater Vehicle" tradition over the Theravada, the so-called Hinayana or "Lesser Vehicle."

It has been difficult for scholars to determine how much historical truth there is in this story, but in any case it's essential to distinguish the bodhisattva ideal from such doctrinal claims. Today we need to understand the bodhisattva path as a nonsectarian archetype that offers a new vision of the relationship between spiritual practice and social engagement—an alternative to rampant self-centered individualism, which can include preoccupation with one's own personal awakening.

According to the usual mythology, bodhisattvas are self-sacrificing because they could choose to transcend this world of samsara by entering into nirvana and ending rebirth, but instead they take a vow to hang around here in order to help the rest of us. That kind of altruism still distinguishes the best interests of the bodhisattva from the best interests of everyone else. There is a better way to understand what motivates the bodhisattva—if we understand awakening as the realization that I am not separate from (the rest of) the world. Then the bodhisattva's preoccupation with helping "others" is not a personal sacrifice but a further stage of personal development. Because awakening to my nonduality with the world does not automatically eliminate habitual self-centered ways of thinking and acting, following a bodhisattva path becomes important for reorienting my relationship with the world. Instead of asking, "What can I get out of this situation?" one asks, "What can I contribute to this situation, to make it better?"

Thus the bodhisattva path is a way of emphasizing the important distinction between two basic ways of understanding the Buddhist path: do I follow the path only to end my own suffering, or to address the suffering of everyone?

That speaks directly to an important tension today between "self-help" Buddhism and socially engaged Buddhism. Many if not most North American Buddhists have demanding jobs, and practices such as *metta* and mindfulness meditation provide much-needed relief from the pressures of daily life. Such practitioners seek quiet time to de-stress and pursue their own enlightenment, or at least their own peace of mind.

Without denigrating in any way the importance of such practice, we also need to remember Slavoj Zizek's criticism that Buddhism can be practiced in ways that reinforce the current social order. Is Western Buddhism being commodified and co-opted into a self-help stress-reduction program that adapts to institutionalized dukkha, leaving practitioners atomized and powerless? Or is modern Buddhism opening up new perspectives and possibilities that challenge us to transform ourselves and our societies, so that they become more socially just and ecologically sustainable?

Among those who recognize the importance of social engagement, there is another distinction to be made. My sense is that most Buddhists understand social engagement as serving the underserved, as directly responding to those who need help, such as homeless people, those who are terminally ill, or those incarcerated in prisons. This seems consistent with Buddhist emphasis on letting go of abstractions in favor of immediate experience: attending to the needs of that suffering person on the sidewalk, right here and now, rather than becoming involved in a more abstract and sometimes confrontational movement for social change.

Again, without disparaging in any way the importance of helping those who urgently need it, we must also ask: if we share the basic concern of the Buddha to end suffering, don't we also need to understand and address its social causes? As we pull drowning people out of the river, shouldn't we consider why there are an increasing number of people floundering in the water? Who or what is pushing them in upstream? Today it's not enough to help that homeless person in front of us. We also need to consider why, in the wealthiest and most powerful nation in human history, the number of poor people is growing so quickly. In particular, why (to cite some recent statistics) are over a million schoolchildren homeless in the U.S.? Why are a quarter of our children growing up in poverty—the second-highest percentage among developed nations (after Romania), according to a 2014 UNICEF report?

> When I give food to the poor, they call me a saint.
> When I ask why they are poor, they call me a communist.
> —DOM HELDER CAMARA

So bodhisattva activism is also concerned to address institutional causes of dukkha, and it has some distinctive characteristics.

Interdependence—the idea that "we're all in this together"—is one; a focus on delusion rather than evil is another. Together, these imply nonviolence (violence is usually self-defeating anyway) and a politics based on love rather than anger (which dualizes between "us" and "them"). Although it's not always easy to remember, the basic issue is not wealthy and powerful "bad" people but social structures that promote collective greed, aggression, and delusion. The Buddha's pragmatism and nondogmatism—for example, viewing his own teachings as a raft not to be carried on our backs once we've crossed the river—can help to cut through the ideological quarrels that have weakened so many progressive groups. And Buddhist emphasis on skillful means foregrounds the creative imagination, a necessary attribute if we are to co-construct a healthier way of living together on this earth.

> The difficult we do immediately.
> The impossible will take a little longer.
> —THE U.S. ARMY CORPS OF ENGINEERS

Yet those attributes, essential as they are, do not touch on the most important aspect of the bodhisattva path in these difficult times, when we often feel overwhelmed by the magnitude of the challenge. The bodhisattva's response? In the Zen centers where I have practiced, the "four bodhisattva vows" are recited every day, the first of which is "living beings are numberless; I vow to save them all." This accords with the classical formulation: bodhisattvas pledge to help liberate all sentient (literally "breathing") beings. Given the size of the universe, this is no small commitment—and that is my point. Someone who has signed up for such an unachievable task is not going to be intimidated by present crises, no matter how difficult or even hopeless they may appear. That is because the bodhisattva practices on both levels, inner and outer, which enables him or her to engage wholeheartedly in goal-directed behavior without attachment to results.

> Ours is in the trying.
> The rest is not our business.
> —T. S. ELIOT

The task of the bodhisattva is to do the best one can, without know-ing what the consequences will be. Have we already passed ecologi-cal tipping-points and civilization as we know it is doomed? Frankly, we don't know—yet rather than being overawed by the unknown, the bodhisattva embraces "don't know mind," because Buddhist prac-tice opens us up to the awesome mystery of an impermanent world where everything is changing whether or not we notice. I grew up in a world defined by the Cold War between the United States and the Soviet Union, a standoff haunted by the always-imminent possibility of nuclear war. Most of us took this situation for granted—until com-munism suddenly collapsed overnight. The same thing occurred with South African apartheid. If we do not really know what's happening, do we really know what's possible, until we try?

The equanimity of the bodhisattva-activist is due to nonattachment to the fruits of one's action, which is not the same as detachment from the state of the world or the fate of the earth. Nonattachment does not mean that one is unconcerned about the results of one's activism, yet it is essential in the face of the inevitable setbacks and frustrations that activism involves, which otherwise lead to simmering anger, despair, and burnout. Given the urgency of the challenges, we work as hard as we can. When our efforts do not bear fruit in the ways that we hoped, we naturally feel some disappointment—but we do not remain stuck there, because we have an inner practice that helps us not to hold on to such feelings.

What is the source of the bodhisattva-activist's nonattachment? That points to the fruits of his or her inner work: the bodhisattva realizes shunyata "emptiness," the dimension where there is nothing to gain or lose, no getting better or worse. The Diamond Sutra says, in effect, that we save all living beings by realizing that there are no living beings to save. That is a very important realization, although it is not by itself the full awakening that we need.

Shunryu Suzuki used to tell his students "you're all perfect just as you are... and you can use a little improvement." Both are completely true. Part II mentioned the danger, for practitioners, of becoming attached to that insight ("clinging to emptiness"). To say it again, emptiness is not a place to dwell that is free from form; it is experienced in or as the impermanent forms it takes, which include our world and our own lives. In terms of the "new story," realizing shunyata opens us up to the source of the creative process, liberating a creativity that is much needed today.

For the Buddhist activist these are the two complementary dimensions of practice, which turn out to be different sides of the same coin. As Nisargadatta might put it, "Between these two the bodhisattva's life turns." Our world needs both.

CONCLUSION:

Reflections on Karma and Rebirth

WHETHER BUDDHISM is a religion, a philosophy, a psychology, a spiritual path, or a way of life—or all the above—its main teachings seem remarkably modern. Their emphasis on impermanence and interdependence parallels contemporary theories of evolution and ecology. The teachings on insubstantiality have echoes in physics, the emphasis on the deceptions of language mirrors a main concern of modern philosophy, and the notion that the sense of self is constructed and conditioned aligns with developmental psychology. Notably, however, these many similarities do not include karma as an inexorable moral law built into the cosmos; nor do they mention karma's traditional corollary, physical rebirth. Both have been very important if not essential to all Asian Buddhisms. But what can they mean for us today? How do they fit into a more contemporary understanding of the Dharma?

It may seem strange that a book devoted to presenting a more modern version of Buddhism has not had more to say about karma and rebirth. In fact, much of this book has been about karma and rebirth, despite not using those terms.

The basic issue with both, from a contemporary perspective, is that they are unfamiliar and alien to the current worldview. They're also inconsistent with the prevailing materialistic paradigm of modern science, which has discovered no mechanism that might explain them.

Whether or not that is sufficient for contemporary Buddhists to doubt them, there are other issues. The karma teaching has often been commodified into an emphasis on acquiring merit; this promotes a form of spiritual materialism more interested in earning a favorable rebirth than in putting an end to dukkha—whether one's own or another's. As noticed earlier, karma has also been used to rationalize and accept social injustice. The conventional Buddhist understanding of one's own karmic stream as individual and discrete is normally taken to mean that I am ultimately responsible for whatever happens to me: it is the result of my earlier volitional actions. This kind of thinking, taken to its "logical" conclusion, can lead one to wonder about the awful personal karma each Jew must have had to be born into Nazi Germany. And all the Dalit "untouchables" who are still oppressed in India today must also deserve their fate.

For these reasons, the karma-and-rebirth doctrine is one of the most important issues for contemporary Buddhism. Must we accept it, if we want to be Buddhists? Must we reject it, if we want to be modern? It becomes a touchstone for the dialogue between the two: can we engage in a genuine conversation that is not predisposed to disprove one side or the other? The answer to that question has important consequences for the future of a globalizing Buddhism.

Although karma and rebirth were already widely accepted in pre-Buddhist India, Brahminical teachings understood them more mechanistically: performing a Vedic sacrifice properly would sooner or later lead to the desired consequences, if not in this lifetime then in the next. The Buddha transformed this ritualistic approach into a moral principle by focusing on volitions and motivations. As the *Dhammapada* emphasizes in its opening verses:

> Experiences are preceded by mind, led by mind, and produced by mind. If one speaks or acts with an impure mind, suffering follows even as the cart-wheel follows the hoof of the ox.... If one speaks or acts with a pure mind, happiness follows like a shadow that never departs.

The term *karma* literally means "action." According to popular understanding, the law of karma is a way to get a handle on what will happen to us sometime in the future, but to focus on the eventual consequences of our actions puts the cart (effect) before the horse (action) and misses the revolutionary significance of the Buddha's insight. Karma is better understood as the simple—although not necessarily easy—key to personal transformation: my life situation can be transformed by reforming what *motivates* my actions right now, and by making those volitions habitual.

This brings us back to the crucial role of the sankhara, the mental tendencies discussed in part I. Whether habitual mental tendencies are the result of repeated intentional actions in past lifetimes or childhood conditioning in this lifetime, the important point is that they can be changed. Part I discussed the *deconstruction* of self that happens when we meditate; transforming one's engrained motivations is about the *reconstruction* of self. If the sense of self is composed of mostly habitual ways of thinking, feeling, acting and reacting, and so forth, what are its most important components? Which sankhara play the greatest role in affecting how I relate to other people? To change my motivations is to experience the world in a different way. And when I respond differently to the opportunities the world presents to me, the world is likely to respond differently to me.

Our ways of acting involve feedback systems that incorporate other people. If I am motivated by greed, ill will, and delusion, I must manipulate the world to get what I want, playing a game in which my true intentions are disguised. This reinforces the basic problem at the root of my dukkha: my sense of separation from others. Inevitably I feel more alienated from other people, and they feel more alienated from me when they realize what's going on. On the other side, when my actions are motivated by generosity, loving-kindness, and the wisdom of interdependence, I can relax and open up to the world. The more I feel genuinely connected with other people, the less I will be inclined to use and abuse them, and consequently the more inclined they will be to trust and open up to me.

From this perspective, we experience karmic consequences not so much for what we have done as for what we have become, and what we intentionally do is what makes us what we are. In other words, we are "punished" not for our "sins" but *by* them. And, on the other side, happiness is not the reward for virtue; happiness is virtue itself, as Spinoza put it.

Another way to say it is that karma is not something the self *has*; rather, it is what the sense of self *is*, because my sense of self is transformed by my conscious choices. Just as my body is composed of the food eaten and digested, so "I" am (re)constructed by my consistent, repeated mental attitudes. By choosing to change what motivates me, I change the kind of person I am.

Of course, this more naturalistic understanding of karma is not as deterministic as the traditional version. If you are a Jew caught in Nazi Germany, being a nice guy may not help you very much. Nor does it exclude the possibility of other, perhaps more mysterious possibilities regarding the consequences of our actions. What is clear, however, is that karma as how-to-transform-my-life-situation-by-transforming-my-motivations-right-now is not a fatalistic doctrine but an empowering teaching. Being responsible for what happens to us does not mean accepting passively the problematic circumstances of our lives. Rather, we cultivate the response-ability to improve our situations by addressing them more proactively.

What does this way of understanding karma imply about rebirth?

The notion of rebirth is closely associated with the belief that nirvana involves achieving something transcendent, because otherwise the end of rebirth is difficult to comprehend as anything but nihilism: the end of life and consciousness, period. And that would be a hard sell to most people, even if life in samsara is inevitably bound up with dukkha. So if awakening is not about attaining some "higher dimension," as I have argued, then a different understanding of rebirth and the end of rebirth is needed.

A traditional objection to rebirth is that, if there's no self, what's reborn? The traditional Buddhist answer is: sankhara, one's habitual tendencies, are what survive death and lead to the conception and development of a new psychophysical being, which is necessary for those tendencies to continue actualizing. The sense of self as we know it does not survive, which is why we don't remember our past lifetimes, yet mental tendencies continue to exist, and cause the formation of a new one.

> The stuff of the universe is ultimately mind-stuff.
> What we recognize as the material universe, the universe
> of space and time and evolutionary particles and energies,
> is then an avatar, the materialization of primal mind.
> In that sense, there is no waiting for consciousness to arise.
> It is there always.
> —NOBEL LAUREATE GEORGE WALD, "The Cosmology of Life and Mind"

If, as is widely believed, consciousness is something that arises only when an organism develops to a very complex level of physical organization, then the notion that sankhara survive the physical disintegration of death seems quite implausible. If mind is an epiphenomenon of matter, no "vehicle" for those mental tendencies remains after the body decomposes. That, however, is to assume the prevailing materialistic and reductionist paradigm, which was questioned in part II. If, however, consciousness is basic—if there might be rudimentary awareness even at the quantum level, as some physicists now believe—then there may be some plausibility to the notion of sankhara persisting after bodily death. And that might allow for postmortem karma, in the sense discussed above: it's not that my particular "I" will in future lifetimes continue to experience the results of past actions, but there might still be some causal continuity. Conditioning could continue beyond the grave.

This is very speculative, of course, yet the possibility is attractive— perhaps too attractive. Similar to scientific laws about the conservation of matter and energy, we would like to think that one's character, which has developed over the course of a lifetime, might persist in some fashion. Then there would be not only the evolution of species and cultures—which both continue despite the death of the individuals involved—but also the evolutionary development of what was described in part II as human epicenters of cosmic creativity.

How far does one want to go with such conjectures? I am reminded of the Buddha's warning about metaphysics. In any case, it would be unwise to pin one's belief in karma and rebirth on such speculations.

There are other problems with the very concept of rebirth. For rebirth to occur, there must be some*thing* that is reborn, yet without a self there is no subject (noun) for the predicate (verb) to modify. Indeed, for Buddhism there are only "predicates," since the world is not a collection of things but a confluence of impermanent processes. Although some Buddhist teachers talk about death and rebirth in every moment, as mental and physical events arise and pass away, that can only be a metaphor, since, again, dying and being born are predicates that need a subject to be meaningful. The question remains: who or what is reborn?

In some well-known passages the Buddha refused to speculate on what happens to an awakened person after physical death. He has sometimes been criticized for being evasive about the horrible truth—the finality of death—but that objection misses the significance of many references in the Pali Canon and later Buddhist texts to the Deathless, the Unborn, the Un-disintegrating, and so forth. If these do not refer to something transcendent, what do they refer to?

Near the end of part I, a long quotation from Thomas Traherne (and a much shorter one from William Blake) referred to *something infinite appearing behind everything*. For both of them, infinity is not a theoretical concept, it is something that can be perceived—not by itself, but as characteristic of things. And that is a valuable hint, which I have related to shunyata "emptiness."

We are reminded of the nonduality of form and emptiness, used in part II to understand the relationship between the creative process that *is* the universe and the impermanent forms whereby that process manifests, or *presences*. It is very difficult to discuss form and emptiness without dualizing between them, because language is dualistic and pushes us in that direction. Talking about "emptiness" tends to make it (it!) into a thing that takes form—another thing. And this is precisely where questions about rebirth get into trouble. Will I be reborn after I die, or not? Does an awakened person continue to exist in some way after death, or not? In other words, does this or that predicate apply? All these questions presuppose the self-existence of the subject right now, something Buddhism denies.

To avoid assuming that the nouns form and emptiness refer to things that can be distinguished from each other, it is better to talk about each only in relation to the other. Forms do not have any reality of their own: they are only forms of _____. Of what? What appeared behind everything Traherne saw? Something infinite, which is how we would see everything if our doors of perception were cleansed, according to Blake. How do we cleanse those doors? Well, what did the Buddha recommend to Bahiya in the Honeyball Sutta? "When there is for you in the seen only the seen, in the heard only the heard..."

In Buddhist terms, to experience the shunyata, the emptiness, of the various forms in this world is to perceive them as infinite—and "eternal" too, according to Traherne's understanding of eternity. Yes, I know it makes no sense to talk that way about seeing the infinite, but is the problem with their experience, or with our language?

Let's apply this to the issue of rebirth. From a form perspective, the particular form that is me can be said to have been born on a certain date, in a particular place, and that form will undoubtedly die on another date. From the emptiness perspective, however, I cannot die insofar as "I" was never born. I have no reality or self-existence because I've always been only a form of _____, of what Traherne and Blake describe as the infinite, of what part II described as the cosmic creative process, which is as infinite as anything could be.

To awaken is to realize that—although that way of expressing it isn't quite right, because it's still dualistic. It's not that "I" realize something, but that which takes form as me becomes aware of _____ ... no, that way of putting it isn't much better. Emptiness wakes up to its true nondwelling nature. The bottom falls out of the bucket and mind comes forth without fixing itself anywhere. Let's leave it at that.

From that perspective we can say that there is *only* rebirth: the "empty" creative process of the cosmos incessantly generating new forms by recycling old ones. What looks to us like death is necessary for that to happen. Individual physical immortality—the dream of transpersonalists—would be disastrous. Old forms need to make way for new ones.

What does that mean personally? When "I" die, will there continue to be some kind of (nondual?) experience? Or will physical death be the end of experience, for "me" anyway? What did the Buddha say?—or rather, what did he refuse to say?

The end of part III discussed the "awakened activism" of the bodhisattva, who acts without knowing whether anything he or she does will make any difference whatsoever. She can do this because of her dual practice: continuing the path of personal transformation (for example, meditation) while doing everything she can to promote social and ecological transformation. The two types of transformation reinforce each other. The more deeply she realizes her nonduality with the world and the earth, the more she feels called to respond to its dukkha, and the more she does so, the more her self-centered sankhara transmute into compassionate mental tendencies.

And what about when it comes time for her to die? Does something survive, or…?

Even as her job is to do the best she can, not knowing whether it makes any difference, so for her it makes no difference whether death is the end of her experience, or not. She doesn't know, and she doesn't need to know: that's not part of the job description. Realizing her "emptiness" is part of the role: she knows she is a manifestation of something greater than herself, which Buddhist texts sometimes describe as Unborn and Deathless.

In a way, it's the opposite of Pascal's famous wager. Pascal wrote that we should believe in God even if we're not sure, because if there is a God then we have won heaven, and if there is no God we have lost nothing. The Buddhist path is not about that kind of faith: the Buddha wasn't concerned about whether we believe in him, but how we practice and how we live. If there is some kind of life after death, the form that it takes will take care of itself, if we do what we are called to do right here and now. If nothing of that particular form survives death, that's okay too. That which has taken form as her, and you and I, will continue to presence in other ways. In any case, our dual practice opens us up to the satisfaction and joy of being part of that process in the eternal present.

Is that as much of an answer as we need to the question about karma and rebirth?

ACKNOWLEDGMENTS

MANY FRIENDS have helped this book on its way, including Joseph Bobrow, Bhikkhu Bodhi, Grace Burford, David Chernikoff, Paul R. Fleischman, Ruben Habito, Vince Horn, Al Kaszniak, Ian Linn, Tom McFarlane, Philip Novak, Ron Purser, Johann Robbins, Donald Rothberg, Alan Senauke, Mu Soeng, John and Diane Stanley, Mark Sweitzer, and others too numerous to list. None of them is responsible for the misconceptions that remain.

Special thanks to Naropa University for a research fellowship in the fall of 2011, during which I worked on the first draft. I'm also grateful to Josh Bartok, Lydia Anderson, Maura Gaughan, and especially Laura Cunningham at Wisdom Publications, who worked diligently to whip the manuscript into publishable shape. None of them is responsible for the stylistic infelicities that remain.

Earlier versions of some parts of this book were published in *Tricycle*, *Shambhala Sun*, *Buddhadharma*, and *Huffington Post* blogs. In particular, a shorter version of part III was published as "Why Buddhism and the West Need Each Other" in the *Journal of Buddhist Ethics* and the *Journal of Buddhist-Christian Studies*.

I am forever indebted to and inspired by my teachers: Yamada Koun, Robert Aitken, Brigitte D'Ortschy, and Linda Goodhew.

RECOMMENDED BOOKS

Abrams, Nancy Ellen, and Joel R. Primack. *The New Universe and the Human Future: How a Shared Cosmology Could Transform the World.* New Haven: Yale University Press, 2011.

Aronson, Harvey. *Buddhist Practice on Western Ground: Reconciling Eastern Ideals and Western Psychology.* Boston: Shambhala, 2004.

Bhikkhu Bodhi, ed. *In the Buddha's Words: An Anthology of Discourses from the Pali Canon.* Boston: Wisdom Publications, 2005.

Bhikkhu Bodhi, trans. *The Connected Discourses of the Buddha: A Translation of the Samyutta Nikaya.* Boston: Wisdom Publications, 2003.

———. *The Numerical Discourses of the Buddha: A Complete Translation of the Anguttara Nikaya.* Boston: Wisdom Publications, 2012.

Bhikkhu Nanamoli and Bhikkhu Bodhi, trans. *The Middle Length Discourses of the Buddha: A Translation of the Majjhima Nikaya.* Boston: Wisdom Publications, 1995.

Brock, Rita Nakashima, and Susan Brooks Thistlethwaite. *Casting Stones: Prostitution and Liberation in Asia and the United States.* Minneapolis: Augsburg Fortress: 1996.

Burford, Grace G. *Desire, Death, and Goodness: The Conflict of Ultimate Values in Theravada Buddhism.* New York: Peter Lang, 1991.

Carrette, J. and Richard King. *Selling Spirituality: The Silent Takeover of Religion.* London: Routledge, 2004.

Conze, Edward, trans. *Astasahasrika Prajnaparamita.* London: The Asiatic Society, 1958.

Conze, Edward. *Buddhist Thought in India: Three Phases of Buddhist Philosophy.* Ann Arbor: University of Michigan Press, 1967.

Elgin, Duane. *The Living Universe: Where Are We? Who Are We? Where Are We Going?* San Francisco, CA: Berrett-Koehler, 2009.

Fleischman, Paul R. *Wonder: When and Why the World Appears Radiant.* Amherst, MA: Small Batch Books, 2013.

Garfield, Jay L. *The Fundamental Wisdom of the Middle Way: Nagarjuna's Mulamadhyamakakarika.* New York: Oxford University Press, 1995.

Harding, Stephan. *Animate Earth: Science, Intuition, and Gaia.* White River Junction, Vermont: Chelsea Green, 2006.

Hawken, Paul. *Blessed Unrest: How the Largest Movement in the World Came Into Being and Why No One Saw It Coming.* New York: Viking Press, 2008.

Ireland, John, trans. *The Udana and the Itivuttaka: Two Classics from the Pali Canon.* Sri Lanka: Buddhist Publication Society, 1998.

Jones, Ken. *The New Social Face of Buddhism: A Call to Action.* Boston: Wisdom Publications, 2003.

Kauffman, Stuart A. *Reinventing the Sacred: A New View of Science, Reason, and Religion.* New York: Basic Books, 2010.

Kapleau, Philip. *The Three Pillars of Zen: Teaching, Practice, and Enlightenment.* New York: Anchor, 1989.

Ling, Trevor. *The Buddha: Buddhist Civilization in India and Ceylon.* London: Penguin, 1976.

Lipton, Bruce H., and Steve Bhaerman. *Spontaneous Evolution: Our Positive Future and a Way to Get There From Here.* Carlsbad, CA: Hay House, 2010.

Loy, David R. *The Great Awakening: A Buddhist Social Theory.* Boston: Wisdom Publications, 2003.

———. "Healing Ecology." *Journal of Buddhist Ethics* 17 (2010): 253–67.

———. *Money Sex War Karma: Notes for a Buddhist Revolution.* Boston: Wisdom Publications, 2009.

Margulis, Lynn, and Dorian Sagan. *What Is Life?* New York: Simon & Shuster, 1995.

Muller, Herbert. *Freedom in the Ancient World.* New York: Harper, 1961.

Murphy, Susan. *Minding the Earth, Mending the World: Zen and the Art of Planetary Crisis*. Berkeley, CA: Counterpoint, 2014.

Purser, Ron, and David Loy. "Beyond McMindfulness." *Huffington Post*. Posted 07/01/2013. http://www.huffingtonpost.com/ron-purser/beyond-mcmindfulness_b_3519289.html.

Red Pine, trans. *The Platform Sutra: The Zen Teaching of Hui-neng*. Berkeley, CA: Counterpoint, 2008.

Rothberg, Donald. *The Engaged Spiritual Life: A Buddhist Approach to Transforming Ourselves and the World*. Boston: Beacon, 2006.

Rubin, Jeffrey B. *Psychotherapy and Buddhism: Toward an Integration*. New York: Springer, 1996.

Rue, Loyal D. *Everybody's Story: Wising Up to the Epic of Evolution*. Albany: State University of New York Press, 1999.

Sahtouris, Elisabet. *EarthDance: Living Systems in Evolution*. Bloomington, IN: iUniverse, 2000.

Segall, Seth Robert. *Encountering Buddhism: Western Psychology and Buddhist Teachings*. Albany: State University of New York Press, 2003.

Sheldrake, Rupert. *Science Set Free*. New York: Deepak Chopra Books, 2012.

Snyder, Gary. *Earth House Hold*. New York: New Directions, 1969.

Swimme, Brian, and Thomas Berry. *The Universe Story: From the Primordial Flaring Forth to the Ecozoic Era—A Celebration of the Unfolding of the Cosmos*. San Francisco: HarperOne, 1994.

Tanahashi, Kazuaki, ed. *Moon in a Dewdrop: Writings of Zen Master Dogen*. San Francisco: North Point Press, 1985.

Thich Nhat Hanh. *Love Letter to the Earth*. Berkeley, CA: Parallax Press, 2013.

Thurman, Robert, trans. *The Holy Teaching of Vimalakirti: A Mahayana Scripture*. University Park, PA: Penn State University Press, 2003.

Traherne, Thomas. *Centuries of Meditations*. Charleston, SC: Nabu Press, 2010.

Traleg Kyabgon Rinpoche. "Empty Splendor." *Buddhadharma*, Fall 2013.

Walshe, Maurice, trans. *The Long Discourses of the Buddha: A Translation of the Digha Nikaya*. Boston: Wisdom Publications, 1995.

Welwood, John. *Toward a Psychology of Awakening: Buddhism, Psychotherapy, and the Path of Personal and Spiritual Transformation*. Boston: Shambhala, 2002.

Wilber, Ken. *Quantum Questions: Mystical Writings of the World's Great Physicists*. Boston: Shambhala, 2001.

Zizek, Slavoj. "The Buddhist Ethic and the Spirit of Global Capitalism." Lecture at the European Graduate School, Saas-Fee, Switzerland, August 10, 2012. http://www.egs.edu/faculty/slavoj-zizek/articles/the-buddhist-ethic-and-the-spirit-of-global-capitalism/.

INDEX

A

Abrahamic traditions, 5
  Adam and Eve story, 46, 107
  cosmological dualism, 19–20
  men-over-women hierarchy, 24
  on morality (good vs. evil), 21–22,
    107–8
  on social justice, 105
Abrams, Nancy Ellen, 100
accommodation of Buddhism with the
  state, 116–17
acquiring things outside ourselves:
  desire for, 119–20, 124–25
activism, bodhisattva/awakened, 128,
  130–33, 142
Adam and Eve story, 46, 107
adaptive mutation, 84–85
addiction to desire, 16–17
admission of women into the sangha,
  12–13, 115
Advaita Vedanta, 54, 87–88
Agganna Sutta, 74
aggression. *See* ill will
Aitken, Robert, 87
all-self and no-self, 60
ambiguity in Buddhism, 4–6, 7, 9–10
American dream, 120
Amos, 109
Ananda and the admission of women
  into the sangha, 12–13, 115
annihilationism, 39
anxiety, 9, 16–17, 36, 124

Archimedes, 22
arising. *See* conditioned arising
Aronson, Harvey, 26–27, 37
  Buddhist Practice on Western Ground,
    30
Astasahasrika Sutra, 48
Athenian democracy, 22, 24, 112
attachment. *See* healthy attachment;
  nonattachment
Atthakavagga Sutta, 16–17
Aurobindo, Sri, 88
awakened activism. *See* bodhisattva
  activism
awakening (enlightenment), 39, 40, 49,
  87, 129, 141–42
  ambiguity in, 4–6, 7
  collective enlightenment, 103
  desire for as the urge of the universe,
    86, 102
  Dogen on, 20, 51
  of emptiness, 141–42
  experiences of, 53; Dogen's awaken-
    ing, 53, 86
  helping others as, 129
  idealization of, 32
  ignorance vs., 113–18; vs. good vs.
    evil, 114
  letting go of the sense of self, 20,
    51–54, 99
  liberation from the delusion of self
    as, 44

mindfulness and, 34
Nhat Hanh on, 9
Sutta Nipata on, 16
as of the universe, 86–88
the wisdom of, 48
Yamada on, 52
Yasutani on, 53
See also nirvana; nonduality
Axial traditions, 19–26
See also Abrahamic traditions; Buddhism; the Greeks

B
bacteria: intelligence, 84–85
Bahiya and the Buddha, 17, 43, 47, 141
bare perception, 42
becoming, 77
See also evolution
beings:
and buddhas, 49
saving all living beings, 131, 132–33
See also human beings
belief in God, 80, 81, 142–43
belief in the self, 60
Berry, Thomas, 63, 73, 86
The Universe Story, 66, 85
Berry, Wendell, 59
beyond transcendence and immanence, 39–41, 63–64
Beyondananda, Swami, 123
Bhaerman, Steve, 81
Bhikkhu Bodhi, 35
Big Bang, 78
bin Laden, Osama, 109
biological evolution, 79, 82, 83
biology: revolution in, 63
Blake, William, 58, 59, 141
Blessed Unrest (Hawken), 6–7, 127
Bloom, Howard, 96
Bodhi, Bhikkhu, 35
the bodhisattva, 128–29
the collective bodhisattva, 103
equanimity and nonattachment, 132–33
the new bodhisattva, 126–33
bodhisattva activism, 128, 130–33, 142

the bodhisattva path, 92, 99–100, 129–33, 142–43
the bodhisattva vow, 92, 131, 132–33
Brahmajala Sutta, 114
Brahminical teachings on karma-and-rebirth, 136
the brain: meditation and, 102
Brock, Rita Nakashima, 23, 24
Brown, G. Spencer, 86
the Buddha (Shakyamuni), 79
admission of women into the sangha, 12, 115
and Bahiya, 17, 43, 47, 141
and the caste system, 74, 115
creation myth, 74
on death, 140, 142
intention to transform society, 115
on karma-and-rebirth, 136
mythological stories of, 11
on his teachings, 29–30
The Buddha: Buddhist Civilization in India and Ceylon (Ling), 114–15
buddhas: beings and, 49
See also the Buddha
Buddhism, 114–15
accommodation with the state, 116–17
ambiguity in, 4–6, 7, 9–10
as an Axial tradition, 23–24
creation story, 74–75, 75–76
democracy and, 117
and the Dharma, 54–55
Dogen on studying, 51
ecological implications, 6, 63, 123–26
economic implications, 119–23
and evolution, 76–77
Ling on, 114–15, 116
main teachings, 135
new story, 86–90, 103, 133
predicates only in, 140
on progress, 92–94
as a rationalization of capitalism, 34–35, 37–38
and science, 3–4, 6, 75–76
secular. *See* secular Buddhism
secular society and, 117

and social dukkha, 35, 106, 119–21
social implications, 6–7, 63, 106,
    119–23
socially engaged Buddhism, 106
and structural dukkha, 116–17, 121–23
and Western civilization, 1–7, 117
worldview, 74, 77
Buddhist practice:
    basic practices, 47–48
    without Buddhist roots. See secular
        Buddhism
    deconstruction of the self and the
        world, 41, 42–43, 47–48, 51, 56–57
    dispassion, 50–51
    goal. See goal of Buddhist practice
    koan practice: Mu, 51–53
    letting go of the sense of self, 20,
        51–54, 99
    mindfulness movement vs., 5, 10, 26,
        33–38, 39
    motivations of, 37
    need for, 102
    psychotherapy vs., 5, 26–33, 39,
        39–40
    reconstruction of the self, 137–38
    self-preoccupation in, 37; healthy
        attachment, 31–32
    See also meditation; mindfulness;
        nonattachment
Buddhist Practice on Western Ground
    (Aronson), 30
Burford, Grace: Desire, Death, and Good-
    ness, 16–17
Bush, George W., 109
bypassing, spiritual, 32

C
Cairns, John, 84
Camara, Dom Helder, 130
Campbell, Joseph, 18, 36, 65, 66, 76, 82
Canki Sutta, 29–30
capitalism:
    Buddhism as a rationalization of,
        34–35, 37–38
    and creativity, 97
    rationalization of, 71–72

Carnegie, Andrew, 69
Carrette, Jeremy, 35
caste system: the Buddha and, 74, 115
Centuries of Meditations (Traherne),
    55–56, 60
the challenge (for humans):
    as cognitive, 101–2, 114, 120–21, 123
    ecological aspects, 6, 63, 123–26
    economic and social aspects, 6–7, 63,
        106, 119–23
    of social transformation, 126–27
    See also good vs. evil
Cleisthenes, 111
climate change, 25, 122
cognitive realization, 22
    as the answer to the basic problem
        and challenge for human beings,
        101–2, 114, 120–21, 123
the collective bodhisattva, 103
collective enlightenment, 103
collective selves, 121, 124
commandments of God, 107
compassion: and self-value, 37
    See also loving-kindness
conditioned arising, 41
    evolution/becoming as, 77, 79
consciousness, 41, 84, 139
    as agency, 62
    freedom and, 80
    human beings as the consciousness
        of the earth/universe, 65, 83, 85, 86,
        94–95, 97–98, 100
    vs. matter, 22, 81
    of one "gone out," 15
    self-consciousness, 46, 107
    See also mind; sense of lack; sense of
        meaning/place/role; sense of self
construction of the self and the world,
    40–41, 41–47, 56, 62, 119
consumerism, 72, 121
    and the sense of lack in oneself,
        119–20, 123
Conze, Edward, 2
    on deconstruction, 43
    on perception, 42
corporate cultures: stress in, 35

corporate fixation on profitability and
growth, 121–22, 124–25
corporate mindfulness. *See* mindfulness
movement
corruption as delusion, 61
cosmological dualism, 19–20, 21–23, 59
in social hierarchies, 24–25
within us, 23–24
countertransference, 27
creation stories/myths, 73–76
Buddhist story, 74–75, 75–76
new paradigm/story/myth of cosmology and evolution, 65, 66, 73, 76–86
creativity:
capitalism and, 97
evolution as, 81
and freedom, 100–1
of human beings, 94–97, 140
of nonhuman species, 95
not knowing yet knowing, 89–90
the universe as, 77–78, 88
See also process (of evolution and
creativity)
crisis of our time, 66, 100–3, 109,
111–12, 118–19, 126–27
cultural evolution, 79

D
Dalai Lama, 75
dance of evolution, 81, 81–82
Darling, David, 102
Darwin, Charles: and the disappearance of God from the world, 67–68
Dawkins, Richard: *The Selfish Gene*, 72
Deacon, Terrence, 95
death:
the Buddha on, 140, 142
and deathlessness, 57
as irrelevant, 142–43
persistence of sankhara after, 138–40
and rebirth, 142
deconstruction of the self and the
world, 41, 42–43, 47–48, 51, 56–57
DeLillo, Don, 109
delusion, 17, 101–2, 106
corruption as, 61

institutionalization of, 37, 121
rationalization of, 71
See also ignorance; sense of self
democracy:
Athenian democracy, 22, 24, 112
and Buddhism, 117
without personal reconstruction, 112
the sangha as a democracy, 115–16
Demosthenes, 112
Descartes, Rene, 23
"I think therefore I am," 43–44
Desire, Death, and Goodness (Burford),
16–17
desire:
for acquiring things outside ourselves,
119–20, 124–25
addiction to, 16–17
to awaken as the urge of the universe,
86, 102
See also motivations
devotion to a teacher: idealization of,
32
Dhammapada, 136
the Dharma:
Buddhism and, 54–55
as not refuge, 48
Diamond Sutra, 49, 132–33
Digha Nikaya, 114
direction in evolution, 91, 92
disappearance of God from the world,
25, 67–68
disidentification capability of humans,
99
dispassion, 50–51
Dobzhansky, Theodosius, 81, 91
Dogen Kigen, 2
on awakening, 20, 51
awakening of, 53, 86
on studying Buddhism, 51
See also Shobogenzo
don't know mind, 132
doubting oneself, 43
Dowd, Michael, 101
duality, 108
See also cosmological dualism; good
vs. evil; nonduality

dukkha (suffering), 9, 106, 114
  approaches to. *See* immanence;
    transcendence
  cause/source, 5, 19, 43, 119
  deepest form, 36
  end of. *See* end of suffering
  See also social dukkha; structural
    dukkha
dwelling "in-between," 29
dysfunctional worldview of today, 66
Dyson, Freeman, 80

E
the earth: human beings as the con-
    sciousness of, 65
  See also the world
EarthDance (Sahtouris), 82–83
ecological implications of Buddhism, 6,
    63, 123–26
economic growth: investor and corpo-
    rate fixation on, 121–22, 124–25
economic implications of Buddhism,
    119–23
economics today, 118–19
Einstein, Albert, 79, 80
Elgin, Duane, 78, 89
Eliot, T. S., 132
emptiness:
  awakening of, 141–42
  experiencing, 133
  form and. *See* form and emptiness
  manifestation of, 57–59
  progress from the perspective of, 93
  of the sense of self, 45
  shunyata as, 88
  See also infinity
emptiness and appearance: nonduality
    of, 58–59, 140–42
end of suffering, 10, 15, 17–18, 43,
    50–51
  See also awakening; nirvana
ending rebirth, 16
energy flow, 81
Engler, Jack, 32
enlightenment. *See* awakening

entering the Kingdom of God, 56,
    57–58, 60–61
entrancement, 43
equanimity of the bodhisattva, 132
eternalism, 39
eternity: manifestation of, 57
ethical requirement, 21–22
ethics (morality):
  commandments of God, 107
  good vs. evil, 107–13
  the precepts, 113–14
  secular ethics, 75
  worldviews and, 75
Eurocentrism vs. Orientocentrism, 28
  cross-cultural inquiry, 30
everyday mind, 50
evolution:
  biological evolution, 79, 82, 83
  Buddhism and, 76–77
  as conditioned arising, 77, 79
  as creativity, 81
  cultural evolution, 79
  as a dance, 81, 81–82
  direction in, 91, 92
  mechanistic/reductionist model,
    72–73, 73, 80, 82–83
  need of vision of, 76
  new paradigm/story/myth, 65, 66, 73,
    76–86
  progress in, 90–94
  public disconnect from, 76, 80
  as self-organizing, 81–82, 83–85
  the universe as, 77–78, 88
  See also process (of evolution and
    creativity)
experiences of enlightenment, 53
  Dogen's, 53, 86
experiencing emptiness, 133
experiencing the One, 87–88
experiencing the world as yourself, 5,
    52–54, 55–56

F
fame: our obsession with, 47, 124–25
Fleishman, Paul R., 81, 87, 94
forgetting oneself, 20, 51, 87

form: progress from the perspective of,
93–94
form and emptiness: nonduality of,
58–59, 140–42
Fossella, Tina, 27–28
Foster, Lynn, 21
four Noble Truths, 106
fractal universe, 78
free will, 44
freedom:
and consciousness, 80
and creativity, 100–1
from the delusion of self, 44; vs. for
the self, 118
from religious authority, 67
and security, 124
Freedom in the Ancient World (Muller),
112

G
Gandharan birch bark scrolls, 13–14
Gandhi, Mahatma, 79, 113
vs. Hitler, 93, 94
gap between rich and poor in the U.S.,
111–12, 118–19
rationalization of, 118, 119
Gecko, Gordon, 72
generosity, 106, 137
Genjokoan (*Shobogenzo*), 51
goal of Buddhist practice, 7, 16, 34, 105
Buddhist practice without. *See* secular Buddhism
instrumentalism as subversive of, 36
goals, institutional. *See* institutional
goals
God, 22
belief in, 80, 81, 142–43
commandments, 107
disappearance from the world, 25,
67–68
Einstein on, 80
Hindu proverb on, 80
and the mechanistic model of evolution, 83
See also Kingdom of God
good vs. evil, 107–13

ignorance vs. awakening vs., 114
inquisitions, 108–9
See also social justice concerns/
movements
Gould, Steven Jay: on progress in evolution, 90, 91
greatness of human beings (Nietzsche),
101
greed, 17, 106
desire for acquiring things outside
ourselves, 119–20, 124–25
institutionalization of, 37, 120, 121–22
as "never enough," 121, 125
philosophy of (social Darwinism),
68–73
rationalization of, 71
See also consumerism
the Greeks:
Athenian democracy, 22, 24
social constructivism, 106, 110–11,
124
Greenspan, Alan, 70
growth, economic: investor and corporate fixation on, 121–22, 124–25
Guth, Alan, 78

H
Hakuin Zenji, 49, 51, 89
Hall, Barry, 84–85
happiness, 136, 138
determinants of, 120
hatred. *See* ill will
Hawken, Paul: *Blessed Unrest*, 6–7, 127
healthy attachment:
vs. nonattachment, 31–32
self-preoccupation in Buddhist
practice, 37
Heart Sutra, 58
Hebrew prophets, 105, 109–10, 119
hedonism, 72
helping others as awakening, 129
Hindu proverb on God, 80
Hinüber, Oskar von, 14
Hitler, Adolph, 109
Gandhi vs., 93, 94
Ho, Mae-Wan, 84

Hofstadter, Richard, 69

Holmes, Oliver Wendell, 69

Honeyball Sutta, 17, 43, 141

Huang Po, 50

Hui Hai, 49–50, 108

Huineng: Platform Sutra, 49

human beings:

the basic problem and challenge for
as cognitive, 101–2, 114, 120–21,
123. *See also* delusion; ignorance

as the consciousness of the earth/
universe, 65, 83, 85, 86, 94–95,
97–98, 100

creativity, 94–97, 140

disidentification capability, 99

greatness (Nietzsche), 101

in premodern societies, 98

value/role, 83–84, 94–96. *See also*
sense of meaning/place/role

humanity-over-the-rest-of-nature
hierarchy, 25

hydrogen gas transformation into
matter, 78, 79

I

I am nothing/I am everything, realizing
that, 54

"I think therefore I am" (Descartes),
43–44

ignorance, 43, 48

vs. awakening, 113–18; vs. good vs.
evil, 114

See also delusion

ill will (aggression), 17, 106

institutionalization of, 37, 121

rationalization of, 71

immanence, 5, 10

nirvana as, 16–18, 18–19

the problem with: re the mindfulness
movement, 33–38, 39; re psychotherapy, 26–33, 39, 39–40, 63

and transcendence, 5–6, 38; beyond,
39–41, 59, 63–64

indeterminacy, 80–81

Indian traditions, 22

individual salvation. *See* personal
transformation

individuality: emergence of, 21–22

infinity, 140, 141

manifestation of, 57–58

See also emptiness

inquisitions, 108–9

insecurity of the self, 47

institutional goals: mindfulness movement and, 34–35, 36–37

institutional mindfulness. *See* mindfulness movement

institutional motivations, 121, 122, 123

institutionalization of the three poisons, 37, 121

greed, 37, 120, 121–22

instrumentalism as subversive of the
goal of Buddhist practice, 36

intelligence of bacteria, 84–85

intention:

of the Buddha to transform society,
115

and mindfulness, 34, 36

interdependence, 79

See also conditioned arising

investor fixation on profitability and
growth, 121–22, 124–25

"invisible hand," 71

Isaiah, 109–10

Itivuttaka (Pali text): on nirvana, 14–15

J

James, William, 44

Jaspers, Karl, 19

Jesus, 71, 107–8

on the Kingdom of God, 60–61

parables, 11

Joshu's Mu. *See* Mu

Jung, Carl, 26

just thinking, 44

justice: karma and, 105

See also social justice concerns/
movements

K

Kabat-Zinn, John, 33

Kant, Immanuel, 40–41
karma:
    and justice, 105
    and personal transformation, 137–38
    the sense of self as, 138
    See also karma-and-rebirth
karma-and-rebirth, 135–43
    Brahminical teachings on, 136
    the Buddha on, 136
    rationalization of the status quo, 117
    vs. social justice concerns/move-
        ments, 105–6, 136
    See also karma; rebirth
Kaufmann, Stuart, 82, 84
Kaufmann, Walter, 105
Khuddaka Nikaya, 16
King, Richard, 35
Kingdom of God: entering, 56, 57–58,
    60–61
knowing creativity, not knowing yet,
    89–90
koan practice: Mu, 51–53
Koun Yamada. *See* Yamada Roshi

L
lack (loss): of our sense of meaning/
    place/role, 67, 72–73, 124
    See also sense of lack
language, 42
    limitation of, 141–42
Lao-tse, 93
Lawrence, D. H., 23
Lazlo, Ervin, 83
Leopold, Aldo, 99
letting go of the sense of self, 20, 51–54,
    87, 99
liberation from the delusion of self, 44
life force, 81
Linde, Andrei, 78
Ling, Trevor: on religious traditions and
    Buddhism, 114–15, 116
Lipton, Bruce, 63, 81
loss. *See* lack
love: Nisargadatta on wisdom and, 54
loving-kindness, 16, 106, 137
Luther, Martin, 22

M
Mahakasyapa and Ananda, 13
manifestation of emptiness, 57–59
Mao Zedong, 109
Margulis, Lynn, 84, 85
Marx, Karl, 128
matter:
    consciousness vs., 22, 81
    hydrogen gas transformation into,
        78, 79
    mind and, 80
    mind vs., 62, 81
meaning, sense of. *See* sense of
    meaning/place/role
meaning of the universe, 97–100
mechanistic/reductionist model of
    cosmology and evolution, 72–73, 73,
    80, 82–83
meditation:
    and the brain, 102
    importance, 51
    and psychological problems, 27
men-over-women hierarchy, 24
mental tendencies/dispositions. *See*
    sankhara
metaphors of religious traditions, 18
Metta Sutta, 100
Midgeley, Mary, 73
mind:
    don't know mind, 132
    everyday mind, 50
    and matter, 80
    vs. matter, 62, 81
    nondwelling mind, 4, 49–50, 89
    See also consciousness
Mind and Matter (Schrödinger), 62
mind/body dualism, 23
mindfulness, 34
    and awakening, 34
    without Buddhist roots. *See* mindful-
        ness movement
    intentions and, 34, 36
    the precepts and, 113–14
mindfulness movement (institutional
    mindfulness):

vs. Buddhist practice, 5, 10, 26, 33–38, 39
and institutional goals, 34–35, 36–37
and the sense of self, 36
miracles, three, 78
money: our obsession with, 47, 120, 124–25
Monod, Jacques, 68
morality. *See* ethics
motivations:
  for Buddhist practice, 37
  changing, 137–38
  ego-driven, 17, 112, 113, 126, 136
  institutional, 121, 122, 123
  rationalization of, 71
  See also three poisons
Mozart, 96
Mu (Joshu's Mu), 51–53
Mulamadhyamakakarika (Nagarjuna), 89
Muller, Herbert: *Freedom in the Ancient World,* 112
multiverse, 78
Murphy, Susan, 95
mutation, purposive/adaptive, 84–85
mythological stories of the Buddha, 11
mythology: and science, 76
  See also creation stories/myths; worldviews

N
Nagarjuna: *Mulamadhyamakakarika,* 89
natural world: social convention vs., 110, 124
"never enough," 121, 125
the new bodhisattva, 126–33
new Buddhist story, 86–90, 103, 133
new paradigm/story/myth of cosmology and evolution, 65, 66, 73, 76–86
  as self-organization, 81–82, 83–85
Nhat Hanh, Thich, 9, 77, 103, 120
Nietzsche, 101
Nikayas, 11
  Digha Nikaya, 114
  Khuddaka Nikaya, 16
  Samyutta Nikaya, 17, 50–51

nirvana:
  as immanence, 16–18, 18–19
  the Pali canon on, 11, 14–19
  vs. samsara, 4–5, 10, 15–16
  as transcendence, 15–16, 18, 138
Nisargadatta Maharaj, 54, 133
no-self:
  all-self and, 60
  rationalization of, 32
nonattachment (not clinging), 16, 47–51, 51
  of the bodhisattva, 132–33
  healthy attachment vs., 31–32
  rationalization of, 32
nondualist perspective, 6, 62, 81
nonduality, 20, 25, 38, 49
  all-self and no-self, 60
  of emptiness and appearance, 58–59, 140–42
  experiencing the world as yourself, 5, 52–54, 55–56
  of form and emptiness, 58–59, 140–42
  returning to, 61
nondwelling mind, 4, 49–50, 89
nonhuman species: creativity, 95
not clinging. *See* nonattachment
not knowing: don't know mind, 132
not knowing yet knowing creativity, 89–90

O
omega point, 92
the One: experiencing, 87–88
ordinary mind (everyday mind), 50
organism: the universe as an, 81–82, 83–85
Orientocentrism vs. Eurocentrism, 28
  cross-cultural inquiry, 30
others:
  helping others as awakening, 129
  personal well-being and the well-being of, 37

P
Pali canon:

the bodhisattva in, 128–29
constructivist viewpoint, 41
historical reliability, 10–14
on nirvana, 11, 14–19
on not clinging, 50–51
See also Nikayas
parables of Jesus, 11
Pascal's wager, 142–43
the path:
  bodhisattva path, 92, 99–100, 129–33,
    142–43
  as not exclusively Buddhist, 54–55
  See also Buddhist practice
Paul (the Apostle), 11
perception (seeing process), 41, 41–43
Pericles, 111
persistence of sankhara after death,
    138–40
personal transformation/reconstruction
    (individual salvation), 4–5, 20, 36
  democracy without, 112
  karma and, 137–38
  and social transformation, 7, 37, 64,
    107, 112–13, 117–18, 122–23, 125–26
personal well-being: and the well-being
    of others, 37
physics: revolution in, 62
Platform Sutra (Huineng), 49
Plato, 111, 112
Po Shan, 52–53
power: our obsession with, 124–25
the precepts, 113–14
predicates only in Buddhism, 140
predispositions. *See* sankhara
premodern societies:
  rulers as sacred intermediaries in,
    20–21, 117
  sense of meaning/place/role in, 98,
    124
  social hierarchies in, 24–25, 124
presence, 58–59, 61–62, 63, 140–41
Prigogine, Ilya, 40, 99
Primack, Joel E., 100
the problem (for humans):
  as cognitive, 101–2, 114, 120–21, 123
  our sense of lack as, 46

See also delusion; ignorance
problem with immanence:
  re the mindfulness movement, 33–38,
    39
  re psychotherapy, 26–33, 39, 39–40,
    63
problem with transcendence, 19–26,
    39–40, 63
process (of evolution and creativity):
  explanations of, 80–83
  three stages of, 78–80
  the world/universe as, 56–57, 77–78,
    88, 140
profitability: investor and corporate
    fixation on, 121–22
progress:
  in evolution, 90–94
  social progress, 111
psychological problems: meditation
    and, 27
Psychotherapy and Buddhism (Rubin),
    28–29, 30
psychotherapy vs. Buddhist practice, 5,
    26–33, 39, 39–40
purity, 108
purposive mutation, 84–85

R
radiance of things as they are, 56–57
Rand, Ayn, 70
randomness, 80–81
rationalization:
  of capitalism, 71
  of the delusion of a separate self, 71
  of the gap between rich and poor in
    the U.S., 118, 119
  of motivations, 71
  of no-self/nonattachment, 32
  of the status quo, 34–35, 36, 37–38,
    117, 129–30
reality:
  solipsism, 60
  things as they are, 56–57
  the world as, 59
  See also creativity; nonduality

realization. *See* awakening; cognitive
   realization
realizing that *I am nothing/I am every-*
   thing, 54
rebirth, 138–42
   ending, 16
   See also karma-and-rebirth
recognition, 42
reconstruction of the self, 137–38
refuge: the Dharma as not, 48
reliance on technology, 125
religious authority: freedom from, 67
religious traditions:
   Axial traditions, 19–26. *See also*
      Buddhism
   Ling on, 114–15, 116
   metaphors, 18
The Republic (Plato), 112
responsibility for the well-being of the
   whole biosphere, taking, 99–100,
   125
returning to nonduality, 61
revolution in physics and biology,
   62–63
Rhodes, Tom, 79
Rockefeller, John D., 69–70
role, human. *See* value/role of human
   beings...
romance: our obsession with, 47
Rubin, Jeffrey, 28
   Psychotherapy and Buddhism, 28–29,
      30
Rue, Loyal, 19, 20, 65, 73, 76, 77
ruler-over-ruled hierarchy, 24–25
rulers as sacred intermediaries, 20–21,
   117

S
Sagan, Dorion, 85
Sahtouris, Elisabet, 63, 81–82
   EarthDance, 82–83
Salomon, Richard, 14
salvation, individual. *See* personal
   transformation
samsara vs. nirvana, 4–5, 10, 15–16
Samyutta Nikaya, 17, 50–51

the sangha:
   admission of women into, 12–13, 115
   as a democracy without caste discrim-
      ination, 115–16
sankhara (tendencies/predispositions),
   41, 42, 44, 137
   persistence after death, 138–40
   transformation of, 137–38, 142
   See also motivations
saving all living beings, 131, 132–33
Schrödinger, Erwin: *Mind and Matter,*
   62
science:
   Buddhism and, 3–4, 6, 75–76
   the greatest discovery, 78
   mythology and, 76
   and social hierarchies, 25
Searle, John, 42
secular Buddhism, 3–4, 33–34
   mindfulness movement, 5, 10, 26,
      33–38, 39
   psychotherapy, 5, 26–33, 39, 39–40
secular ethics, 75
secular society:
   and Buddhism, 117
   and the sense of lack in oneself,
      46–47
secular universe, 68
security: and freedom, 124
   See also sense of meaning/place/role
seeing process (perception), 41, 41–43
seeing things as they are, 56–57
the self:
   all-self and no-self, 60
   anxiety, 9, 16–17, 36, 124
   belief in, 60
   construction of, 40–41, 41–47, 56,
      62, 119
   deconstruction of, 41, 42–43, 47–48,
      51, 56–57
   doubting oneself, 43
   experiencing the world as yourself, 5,
      52–54, 55–56
   forgetting oneself, 20, 51, 87
   freedom from the delusion of vs. for
      the self, 118

healing vs. insight into the sense of, 30
insecurity, 47
reconstruction of, 137–38
sense of. See sense of self
sense of lack in. See sense of lack in oneself
See also collective selves
self-consciousness, 46, 107
self-help Buddhism vs. socially engaged Buddhism, 129–30
See also mindfulness movement; psychotherapy vs. Buddhist practice
self-nature: the universe as, 89
self-organization of the universe, 81–82, 83–85
self-preoccupation in Buddhist practice, 37
healthy attachment, 31–32
self-value: compassion and, 37
The Selfish Gene (Dawkins), 72
Selling Spirituality (Carrette and King), 35
sense of lack in oneself, 32, 45–46, 107, 119–20
consumerism and, 119–20, 123
secular society and, 46–47
sense of meaning/place/role:
our lack/loss of, 67, 72–73, 124
in premodern societies, 98, 124
sense of self (delusion of a separate self), 5, 7, 19, 25, 41, 45, 101–2
all-self and no-self, 60
as assumed by eternalism, annihilationism, transcendence, and immanence, 39–40
awakening from, 118
development of, 44–45
emptiness, 45
freedom from, 44; vs. freedom for the self, 118
healing the self vs. insight into, 30
as karma, 138
letting go, 20, 51–54, 87, 99
the mindfulness movement and, 36
overcoming, 17–18

rationalization of, 71
seeing through, 34
separation between church and state, 117
serenity, 16
Shakyamuni. See the Buddha
Shobogenzo (Dogen), 53
Genjokoan, 51
shunyata, 88–89
Skilling, Jeffrey, 72
Smith, Adam: "invisible hand," 71
Snyder, Gary, 105
social constructivism:
of the Buddha, 74
of the Greeks, 106, 110–11, 124
See also social transformation
social convention vs. the natural world, 110, 124
social Darwinism, 68–73
social dukkha, 35, 110
Buddhism and, 35, 106, 119–21
See also structural dukkha
social hierarchies:
in Axial traditions, 24–25
in pre-Axial societies, 124
science and, 25
social implications of Buddhism, 6–7, 63, 106, 119–23
social justice concerns/movements, 105, 109–13, 119, 120–21, 122–23, 127–28
karma-and-rebirth teaching vs., 105–6, 136
See also social dukkha; structural dukkha
social progress, 111
social transformation, 6–7
challenge of, 126–27
personal transformation/reconstruction and, 7, 37, 64, 107, 112–13, 117–18, 122–23, 125–26
the three poisons vs., 106, 112, 121
socially engaged Buddhism, 106, 127
the bodhisattva path, 92, 99–100, 129–33
vs. self-help Buddhism, 129–30

society:
  the Buddha's intention to transform,
    115
  secular society and the sense of lack
    in oneself, 46–47
  See also premodern societies; social...
solipsism, 60
Spencer, Herbert, 68, 69
spiritual bypassing, 32
spiritual practice: need for, 102
  See also Buddhist practice
Stalin, 109
the state: accommodation of Buddhism
    with, 116–17
status quo: rationalization of, 34–35,
    36, 37–38, 117, 129–30
stories:
  Buddhist creation story, 74–75, 75–76
  creativity of human beings, 94–97
  crisis of our time, 66, 100–3
  good vs. evil, 107–13
  the meaning of the universe, 97–100
  mythological stories of the Buddha, 11
  our need for, 103
  new Buddhist story, 86–90, 103, 133
  new paradigm/story/myth of cosmol-
    ogy and evolution, 65, 66, 73, 76–86
  parables of Jesus, 11
  progress in evolution, 90–94
  social Darwinism, 68–73
  See also worldviews
Stravinsky, 96
stress in corporate culture, 35
structural dukkha, 114–15, 117
  Buddhism and, 116–17, 121–23
studying Buddhism: Dogen on, 51
suffering. *See* dukkha
Suharto, 109
survival of the fittest, 68–69, 69–70
Sutta Nipata, 16
Suzuki, Shunryu, 88
Swearer, Donald, 16
Swimme, Brian, 63, 90
  on the greatest scientific discovery, 78
  The Universe Story, 66, 85

T
taking responsibility for the well-being
    of the whole biosphere, 99–100, 125
Tchaikovsky, 96–97
teacher's help in letting go of the sense
    of self, 53
technology: reliance on, 125
Teilhard de Chardin, Pierre, 92
teleology, 92
tendencies. *See* sankhara
things as they are, 56–57
thinking, just, 44
Thistlethwaite, Susan Brooks, 23, 24
three miracles, 78
three poisons, 17, 34, 106
  institutionalization of, 37, 121; greed,
    37, 120, 121–22
  positive counterparts, 106, 137
  rationalization of, 71
  vs. social transformation, 106, 112, 121
  See also delusion; greed; ill will
Thurman, Robert, 74
Toynbee, Arnold, 1
Traherne, Thomas: *Centuries of Medita-
    tions*, 55–56, 60
Traleg Kyabgon Rinpoche, 58
transcendence, 4–5, 10, 10–19
  and democracy, 22, 24
  and immanence, 5–6, 38; beyond,
    39–41, 59, 63–64
  nirvana as, 15–16, 18, 138
  the problem with, 19–26, 39–40, 63
transference, 27
transformation: the universe as, 77–78
  See also personal transformation;
    social transformation
transhumanism, 23–24
Trigger, Bruce, 21
two truths: progress from the perspec-
    tives of, 93–94

U
Udana (Pali text): on nirvana, 14, 15, 17
United States. *See* gap between rich and
    poor...
the universe:

as an organism, 81–82, 83
awakening as of, 86–88
desire to awaken as the urge of, 86,
  102
experiencing as yourself, 53
human beings as the consciousness
  of, 83, 85, 86, 94–95, 97–98, 100
meaning of, 97–100
as multiverse, 78
as process, 77–78, 88
secular universe, 68
as self-nature, 89
self-organization of, 81–82, 83–85
See also the world
The Universe Story (Berry and
  Swimme), 66, 85
U.S. Army Corps of Engineers, 131

V
value/role of human beings, 83–84,
  94–96
See also sense of meaning/place/role
Vidal, Gore, 70
Vimalakirti Sutra, 48
Voldemort, Lord, 108

W
Wald, George, 62, 139
War on Terror, 109
Weinberg, Steven, 97
well-being of the whole, 37
well-being of the whole biosphere: tak-
  ing responsibility for, 99–100, 125
Wells, H. G., 6
Welwood, John, 31–32
West, Paul, 22
Western civilization: Buddhism and,
  1–7, 117
See also social justice concerns/
  movements
Whitehead, Alfred North, 58
Whitman, Walt, 54, 85
will to live of bacteria, 85

Wilson, David Sloan, 76
Wilson, E. O., 70, 73, 101
  on progress in evolution, 91
Winnicott, Donald, 33
wisdom, 106, 137
  of awakening, 48
  Nisargadatta on wisdom and love, 54
women:
  admission into the sangha, 12–13, 115
  men-over-women hierarchy, 24
the world:
  construction of, 40–41, 41–47, 56, 62
  deconstruction of the self and, 41,
    42–43, 47–48, 51, 56–57
  disappearance of God from, 25, 67–68
  experiencing as yourself, 5, 52–54,
    55–56
  human beings as the consciousness
    of the earth/universe, 65, 83, 85, 86,
    94–95, 97–98, 100
  as process, 56–57, 140
  as reality, 59
  See also the universe
worldviews:
  Buddhist worldview, 74, 77
  dysfunctional mechanistic/reduction-
    ist model, 66, 72–73, 73, 80, 82–83
  and ethics, 75
  new paradigm of self-organization,
    81–82, 83–85
  See also stories
Wright, Robin, 79

Y
Yalom, Irvin, 29
Yamada Roshi, 52
Yang-shan, 53
Yasutani Roshi, 53

Z
Zarathustra (Nietzsche), 101
Zizek, Slavoj, 37, 129–30

ABOUT THE AUTHOR

DAVID ROBERT LOY is a professor, writer, and teacher in the Sanbo Zen tradition of Japanese Zen Buddhism. His articles appear regularly in major journals and Buddhist magazines including *Tricycle*, *Shambhala Sun*, *Inquiring Mind*, and *Buddhadharma*, as well as in a variety of scholarly journals.

David is married to Linda Goodhew, a professor of English literature and language (and coauthor of *The Dharma of Dragons and Daemons*). Many of his writings, as well as audio and video talks and interviews, are available on his website: www.davidloy.org.

MORE BOOKS BY DAVID R. LOY

from Wisdom Publications

Money, Sex, War, Karma: Notes for a Buddhist Revolution
176 pages | $15.95 | ebook $11.62

"A flashy title, but a serious and substantial book."—*Buddhadharma*

The Great Awakening: A Buddhist Social Theory
240 pages | $16.95 | ebook $12.35

"A groundbreaking book from an original thinker."—Melvin McLeod,
editor of *The Best Buddhist Writing* series and *Mindful Politics*

The World Is Made of Stories
128 pages | $15.95 | ebook $11.62

"Loy's book is like the self: layer after layer peels away, and the center is
empty. But the pleasure is exactly in the exploration. At once Loy's most
accessible and most philosophical work."—Alan Senauke for *Tricycle*

A Buddhist Response to the Climate Emergency
with John Stanley and Gyurme Dorje
312 pages | $16.95

"If you read only one Dharma book, make it this one."—*The Mirror*

The Dharma of Dragons and Daemons: Buddhist Themes in Modern Fantasy
with Linda Goodhew
176 pages | $14.95

"Eloquent. Loy and Goodhew find Buddhist truths in contemporary non-Buddhist stories. Pullman's dead are released to become images of interpermeation reminiscient of Thich Nhat Hanh's teachings. Frodo's quest is not to find a treasure or slay a dragon, but to let go. Thus, aspects of Buddhist teachings come alive for children of the West."
—*Inquiring Mind*

ABOUT WISDOM PUBLICATIONS

WISDOM PUBLICATIONS is the leading publisher of classic and contemporary Buddhist books and practical works on mindfulness. Publishing books from all major Buddhist traditions, Wisdom is a nonprofit charitable organization dedicated to cultivating Buddhist voices the world over, advancing critical scholarship, and preserving and sharing Buddhist literary culture.

To learn more about us or to explore our other books, please visit our website at www.wisdompubs.org. You can subscribe to our eNewsletter, request a print catalog, and find out how you can help support Wisdom's mission either online or by writing to:

Wisdom Publications
199 Elm Street
Somerville, Massachusetts 02144 USA

You can also contact us at 617-776-7416 or info@wisdompubs.org.

Wisdom is a 501(c)(3) organization, and donations in support of our mission are tax deductible.

Wisdom Publications is affiliated with the Foundation for the Preservation of the Mahayana Tradition (FPMT).